LUST &
VAINGLORY

*A Close Encounter
with Death and Success*

ANTHONY L. FREEMAN

authorHOUSE®

AuthorHouse™
1663 Liberty Drive
Bloomington, IN 47403
www.authorhouse.com
Phone: 1 (800) 839-8640

Published by AuthorHouse 01/10/2019

ISBN: 978-1-5462-7120-8 (sc)
ISBN: 978-1-5462-7118-5 (hc)
ISBN: 978-1-5462-7119-2 (e)

Library of Congress Control Number: 2018914556

Scripture quotations marked MSG are taken from The Message. Copyright © 1993, 1994, 1995, 1996, 2000, 2001, 2002, 2003 by Eugene H. Peterson. Used by permission of NavPress Publishing Group. Website.

KJV – King James Version
Scripture taken from the King James Version of the Bible.

Contents

Train up a child in the way he should go;
and when he is old, he will not depart from it.
—Proverbs 22:6

Endorsement

Lust is a legitimate desire that's satisfied in an illegitimate manner. The King James Bible says in James 1:14-15: but every man is tempted, when he is drawn away of his own lust, and enticed. Then when lust hath conceived, it bringeth forth sin, and sin when it is finished, bringeth forth death. Succumbing to the spirit of lust has led many astray. There is a place in man that is tailor made specifically for God his creator, nothing else fits so tight and snuggly in the soul of man as does God. In this writing, Lust & Vainglory, Bro. Anthony Freeman tells about his plight of seeking glory for himself, and leaving God out. This book is an interesting read, and it will lock you in so attentively because it speaks to you the individual reader as if it were really your own story. He walks you thru his life-story with passion, not skipping a beat. *This is a must read especially for millennials, and also people from all walks of life who might be seeking the almighty dollar in a hurry.* Bro. Freeman expresses his mistakes, his ebbs and flows, and admonishes us to do things God's way.

Pastor Melvin Brooks

Fairfield Baptist Church

Lithonia, GA

Endorsement

This is candid and a humorous book. As I read this, novel, I found myself laughing and crying at the chain of events that took place. In following the life of Anthony Freeman, I cheered at his successes along with the finding of his wife, Vicki. I praise God that he found Christ in the midst of it all.

If you would like to see one of God's heroes in action, I recommend that you read *'LUST and VAINGLORY: A Close Encounter With Death and Success.'*

Rev. Leon Beeler
Gateway Restoration Church

Morrow, GA

Preface

My motive in writing this autobiography is to encourage and edify those who may be struggling with fear of some form or another. And, the best and most effective way to do that is to first understand what fear is. Fear is that spirit in man that produces apprehension, timidity, fright, and doubtfulness. Fear denotes an emotion that appears to be motivated by threaten evil, impending pain, misinformation, and the unknown. This, in turn, can engulf a person with a desire to avoid a threatening situation or an attempt to escape. At times, one recognizes fear as the initial catalyst that promotes hate and misinformation between races. This spirit called fear impedes progress for millions of people all over the world. A recent poll of about eight hundred people revealed their greatest phobia. It determined that over 65 percent said that their greatest phobia was the fear of dying. Occasionally, some of these people manage to rise above their phobias, while others did not.

Fear comes in various forms and sizes. Whether it is the fear of acceptance by your peers, or the fear of your name called upon in class to respond, fear is plain old fear. Some people fear checking accounts; so instead, they open a savings account and treat it as a checking account. Many have that initial fear of using a computer or some form of modern technology. However, as quoted by others, as well as myself repeatedly, it is human to fear, but it is inhuman to let fear impede progress. So even if you are a person with a small fear, such as being embarrassed or saying something naïve, remember, these fears should be dealt with individually and honestly to determine their power source. I sincerely believe that Christ has enabled me to be more than a conqueror in overcoming the fears that had me bound in my former life struggles. So let Isaiah 41:10 minister unto you as it has to me. Amen.

Fear thou not, for I am with thee: be not dismayed, for I am thy God.
I will strengthen thee; yea, I will help thee: yea, I will uphold thee
with the right hand of my righteousness.

Acknowledgements

I give the honor and the glory to my heavenly father, Jesus Christ, who guided my footsteps in writing this book. I thank you too, mother, for encouraging me with your love and support. May you rest in the peace of the Lord. To my lovely wife, Vicki, and our two boys, Anthony (Ali) and Kareem, I salute you for putting up with me during my late hours at the typewriter. Thank you, Gwendolyn, Kathy, and Vicki for helping proofread this work. May God bless you.

Thank you.

L - R Anthony, Jap, Melvin

Chapter One

CHILDHOOD FEARS

I had waited and waited for this day to arrive, and now that it was finally here, I was terrified. The thought of starting kindergarten had always filled me with great expectations, such as meeting new friends, eating lunch in the cafeteria, and most of all, recess. For some reason, I was having moments of pessimism that I could not explain. I asked myself, "What if I don't make any friends?" Maybe the teacher would appear to be a little strict and unreasonable, and so on. Little did I know that my fears were all vain.

Melvin was next to the eldest child in my family, so he escorted me to school the first day. His being tall, slim, and long in his stride, made it somewhat awkward for me to keep up, but somehow I managed. Melvin encountered little difficulty locating my class, although I had hoped otherwise. He introduced me to my teacher, Miss Cunningham who was short with a rather stocky build, and a very cheerful smile. Melvin said good-bye and departed to his classroom, and I just "boo-hooed". Miss Cunningham was very tactful in calming me down during the moments that passed. I became acquainted with the majority of my classmates, and before the day was out, had more friends than I knew what to do with. From that day forward, kindergarten was smooth sailing for me. All my childhood fear and the accompanying paranoia vanished.

Kindergarten had been a learning experience for me, and the fear of meeting new friends was definitely *a thing of the past*. New friendships continued to develop throughout the summer months. As vacation quickly ended, we made a pact to stick together through thick and thin during the next school year.

It was PTA night and I did not feel good about it; the simple reason was that I had become the leader of a gang. This unsurprisingly created a little mischief around the halls of Frank L. Stanton Elementary School. Some would say that we were headstrong and militant. My teacher, Mrs. Huey, expressed genuine concern to my mother about my involvement in gangs. She said that I was a gifted child and needed to become disassociated, quote unquote, with "gangs". My mother had a talk with me about my poor conduct in school and encouraged me to do better in the future.

Months went by and, amazing as it seems, the gangs were

somehow now extinct. My conduct began to measure up to the level of my grades, "A minus". Although the gangs had ended, there were still a few who looked up to me and thought I had all the answers. For instance, if I did not eat in the cafeteria, they did not either. If I hung out in the halls, they did, too, and so on. At times, it was irritating and repetitious. I suppose that it was the telltale signs of mental growth or perhaps it could have been that my attention had diverted elsewhere. And, it certainly was.

There were two diversions in action, one named Monique and the other named Terrie. Monique had a fair complexion, with beautiful smooth skin, average length semi-dark hair, and her unexpected dimples were a welcoming addition to her cuteness. Terrie, on the other hand, was every guy's dream girl; at least, that is what society dictated. She was quite a pretty picture to look at, and very photogenic. Her creamy light complexion complemented her coal-black silky hair. To be as young as she was, her character soon exceeded expectations.

Monique and Terrie were close, knew each other's likes and dislikes. They were beautiful girls with a pleasing aggressiveness about them that I liked, though at that time I was too young to grasp it fully. Terrie had a thing for boys, especially those who neatly styled their hair with a part in it, and she made it known to my two best friends, Reginald and William, and me. We would discuss our hairstyles, as well as what greasy kid stuff had the best results. We practically lived in the mirror combing, brushing, and styling our hair, preparing for the following school day. Can you imagine kids in first grade carrying on like this? It makes you wonder what we would be doing at age ten.

1

Monique was not as hard to please. She knew what she wanted, saw it, and went after it. One day after school, I changed clothes and went out to play touch football with the neighborhood boys. After catching and throwing a few passes, I noticed a car pull up to one of my neighbor's' house. I continued to throw the ball back and forth until I caught a glimpse of a woman getting out of the car. It was the school's patrolwoman, who was also Monique's mother. I watched her as she entered my neighbor's house; then we resumed our game, that is, until I ran for a long pass near the car and I heard a voice say, "Come here, darling, and give me a kiss".

I could feel my body tense all over. I had to think fast, so I ignored the comment completely and continued to run for the pass. I caught the ball and headed back. As I passed the car, I heard the voice say, "Come here, sugar-dumplin", and talk to your baby." The voice sounded sweet and, oh, so mellow. I could not resist it any longer. I looked in the car and saw Monique and her two sisters.

"Oh, hi, Monique," I said.

"Hello Anthony, come here and give me a kiss, my boyfriend", I was shocked and embarrassed, and so I hurried away quickly before the other guys could realize what was happening.

One of the guys said, "Andy, who is she talking to?'

I replied, "Man, I don't know. C'mon, let's play ball."

Then she yelled out, "Anthony, darling, I love you".

The guys dropped the ball and said, "Let's get 'im."

I ran as fast as I could, but to no avail. They caught me.

I wondered why Monique's mother had not come out yet. If she would just come out, then it would be all over. Of course, I did not have any such luck. The fellows picked me up and hand-delivered me to the car window, and she kissed me, I was so embarrassed that I turned purple. Everybody laughed and we finally resumed the game, but the fellows never let me forget that day.

The following day at school, I noticed that Monique went out of her way not to speak to me. I assumed that I had hurt her feelings by responding negatively to her aggressive approach. As time went on, her feelings healed, and we became friends again. She realized that it was nothing personal, but that I was not quite ready for a serious courtship.

Soon school was out, and we had a party to celebrate the coming summer. Before I realized it, summer was over and I was well into my second year of school. I did very well throughout the second grade, and in the end, I had maintained a B plus average.

Anthony Age 6 in Tucker, GA

Chapter Two

HUBCAPS

✳ ✳ ✳

The aroma of barbecue in the air, along with people planning picnics, was an indication that summer had arrived. We generally went to Lake Altoona or Lookout Mountain, because these were particularly great fun resort areas, but this summer we had our vacation at home. Dad had made plans to use the extra money to buy a used Fifty-Seven Dodge that he had had his eye on. You see, Mother and Father had had very little education because back in those days people had to drop out of school to help in the home or in the fields. Daddy had finished the fourth grade and called it quits, while Mother went on to college for about a year or so. For this reason, they had very low-paying jobs and most of the time Dad worked two jobs. At times, it was very difficult for them to make ends meet, but through the grace of God, we survived. We still took time to visit relatives and friends, which was always a treat for me.

It was about ten o'clock in the morning, and I could smell the aroma of bacon and eggs coming from the kitchen. Mighty Mouse had just gone off the television set, and the birds were singing their praises for thanks on such a beautiful day. Things were going so well, until Mother stuck her head in the room and quoted her proverbial phrase, All right, let's get up and get this house cleaned up."

Boy, how that statement burned me up. It seemed like every weekend all the other kids in the neighborhood could get up, eat, and immediately go out and play. *But nooo,* not us. We had to clean the house from top to bottom before going outdoors. However, fate stepped in today, for Daddy had just come back from the car dealer with a beautiful red-and-white Dodge, "wing tipped". When I looked out, I could not believe how long the car was. Daddy's dream had finally become a reality, and spending vacation at home had paid off.

Joy and excitement filled the air, and Jap, the eldest son, got his camera out and took some pictures. Even Mother showed signs of enthusiasm as we went for a ride through Mosley Park. I felt terrific inside and out and was glad we did not take the vacation, that is, if it meant not getting the car. We washed and waxed the car periodically, Daddy bought some real expensive hubcaps for the wheels, and that was the icing on the cake. Those hubcaps drew a lot of attention that seemed to affirm a choice well chosen. I guess one would say that the compliments and the attention they often received made them worth the price.

Summer had ended, and school was about to begin in a week or so. It was the weekend, and we were playing outside with some of our neighborhood friends down the street, named Phillip and Hershel. The sun had almost completely gone down when their mother called out, "Phillip and Hershel, it's time to come in." They departed for home and so did we. Mother was setting the table for dinner and Daddy was asleep when the doorbell rang. It was Mr. Cooks, our next-door neighbor, who usually crossed over into our yard, instead of using the walkway to the steps.

I answered the door, and Mr. Cooks said, "Hi Andy".

I replied, "Hello, Mr. Cooks". Mr. Cooks looked worried and very concerned. I thought he needed some assistance at home or something, until he said, "Andy, tell your daddy that someone is out here trying to steal his hubcaps. I yelled at him to stop, but he is determined to steal them." I thanked Mr. Cooks for his concern and hurried into the bedroom to awaken my dad. Daddy had always been difficult to awaken from a deep sleep, but time was of essence, and I just prayed that he would wake up in time.

I shook him hard and yelled, "Daddy, wake up, someone is trying to steal your hubcaps".

For the first time in I don't know when, Daddy jumped up and said, "Huh?"

Then I repeated the statement. Daddy hurled to his feet quickly and headed to his dresser drawer. I thought to myself maybe he wanted to put on a clean pair of socks since he did not have any on, but I was wrong. He pulled the drawer open and drew out a real .45 automatic pistol. My mouth fell open and my body tensed up, for this was the first time I had ever seen my father with a gun. Other than watching cowboys on television or seeing a police officer on the street, I had not had any exposure to a real weapon before.

My brothers were in their room watching television when they heard me alert Daddy to the news. Jap ran in to join us immediately, and Melvin passed the word to my mother. Before you could say scat, everybody had lined up in the living room behind Daddy, as he slowly eased the door open to catch the thief in action. Just as Mr. Cooks stated, there was someone bent over taking off the hubcaps. He would have gone prior to dad opening the door, but it appeared as though he had difficulty with the last hubcap. Finally, he broke it free, and it fell to the concrete, making a clanging sound. He quickly grabbed it and stood up to leave; only he did not run away.

His feet had shiny objects on them that reflected in the streetlight. We did not realize what they were until he made his first step toward getting away. The shiny objects were skates, of all things, that made a slashing sound as he quickly made his escape. Daddy had the gun loaded, aimed, and ready, and as the thief made his retreat, Dad pulled the trigger. To all of our surprise, nothing happened. The bullet was jammed in the chamber.

Daddy pulled the trigger repeatedly, to no avail, and then shouted, "Dammit, he's *gettin'* away".

Daddy picked up the phone and called the police, and they came out and filed a report. Of course, they never apprehended the thief; *and needless to say*, my dad did not have the hubcaps insured. I could tell that this incident had taken some of the spunk out of Dad, because he really thought the world of those hubcaps. If I had been old enough to work, I would have found a job and bought him a new set. He was so broken spirited that he did not even bother to put new ones in their place.

Chapter Three

ACCIDENT

The autumn leaves were beginning to change colors and fall gracefully to the ground. I loved the sound of the leaves crushing beneath my feet as I walked slowly to school in the brisk morning air. It was the beginning of the new school term, which had kicked off according to schedule. Mrs. Johnson, whom I had heard was very nice, was my third-grade teacher. I could not wait to get started. All of my old classmates had returned and our teacher determined our seating arrangements. You could never speculate whom Mrs. Johnson designated for the desk in front of me. You guessed it, Terrie.

She did not show it, but I knew she was just as excited about it as I was, so I played things rather subtle for a few days, to insure that all thoughts of aggression were out of focus. Then when she could not stand it any longer, she began to open up to me, which was really, what she had wanted to do all along. I was so glad that I had been patient, although it was most difficult. You see, Terrie had the kind of deep dark eyes that would make any guy melt in her arms, and along with that, had an extremely sexy voice to match.

We became close friends, and occasionally, I walked her home, that is, if she did not ride with her mother. The way things were happening so fast, I would have bet my whole cookie jar that she and I would be sweethearts inside of a week together, a week that would remain in my mind for the rest of my life. If I had had any idea of what waited patiently for me in the near future, I would have told her how much I loved her and how she had made my life more meaningful.

As I traced back a few weeks, I remembered how it all began. Three days after the hubcap incident, I was lying around the house with nothing to do. Mom and Dad had gone to work, and Jap and Melvin were visiting some friends. It was just me, the big house *all to myself, to do with as I pleased.* I tried to resist the temptation, but it was overpowering me. Before I knew it, I was in my parents' room and had opened my daddy's drawer and pulled out his gun. Only this was not the gun; he had the night of the hubcap theft, it was a Smith and Wesson Special. It had a long barrel, just like the ones in the cowboy pictures, and boy, was it heavy. Fear was all over me, coupled with excitement, and I fantasized over about four or five "what ifs". I thought *What if a burglar broke in while I was here alone and I had to shoot him. Could I* do *it? What if I accidentally dropped the gun and it went off, wounding me in the foot or even the upper body?* Finally, I thought, *what if I shot myself in the eye.* What a horrible thought to imagine. I quickly suppressed the thought and put the gun back.

Later, when the whole family arrived, we sat down and played Monopoly, a game that we all enjoyed as a family.

Sometimes, the emotions were so high in that game that it was simply pathetic the way we acted; nevertheless, we always came back for more. We retired that night and arose to another day. Mom and Dad had already left when I awakened, which was nothing out of the ordinary. I did not normally rise and shine until eight-thirty or nine o'clock. Mike and Juju were friends of my brothers, and they had stopped by for some reason or another. While they were there, we had a little fun with them.

Jap went to get my dad's gun and pointed it at Mike, playfully of course, and Mike said, "Okay, J-J-Je-erry-y, I was just kidding". We all cracked up with laughter.

Jap lowered the gun and proceeded to put the bullets back into it. Mike and Juju made comments about its length as well as how shiny it was. Juju went to the bathroom and while he was in there, we decided to play a joke on him. My daddy had a real old shotgun, which looked like it was from World War I. I went to his closet, got it out, and opened the bathroom door.

Juju was sitting on the toilet daydreaming, looked up and saw me with the shotgun, and said, "Dammit, Andy, don't point that at me". Again, we all had a laugh; then I put the shotgun up. Mike and Juju finally left, so we went out to play.

Mother had given us instructions as to the chores she wanted completed before she came home, but as usual we would go down the street to play and when we saw her get off the bus, we would run home and try to clean up before she walked in the house. Sometimes it worked, but not very often. Anyway, it started raining and that was as good an excuse as another one to come in out of the rain and do our chores. Friday's traffic was at its worst, which caused Mother to arrive later than usual.

We were watching television, when both Mom and Dad came in at the same time. The house was clean, dishes washed, and dinner was almost ready. Mom was tired but in a good mood, and Dad had nothing on his mind but food. Before getting dressed for dinner, I saw him put a shiny object in his drawer. Dinner was ready ten minutes later, and Jap called out, "Come and get it". Mother had taught Jap and Melvin how to cook and was slowly training me. We ate a hearty meal, talked for a while, and then went to bed. The weekend flew by like a four-engine rocket, and Monday brought forth the beginning of another week.

So much for reminiscing, let us get back to the third week of school. It was Tuesday, a very hot one at that, so I wore my short sleeve plaid shirt to school. After school, I made it a point to come directly home. I wanted to play some baseball. I arrived home at about three-fifteen, and the door was already open. Jap and Melvin were at home when I arrived and were sitting down in the living room cleaning Daddy's shotgun and his .45 automatic. I was shocked at their being in the living room of all places. If Daddy had come home unexpectedly, he would have caught them red-handed, but as the old saying goes, monkey see monkey do. I put my books down and proceeded to joined them.

I was surprised to see the automatic. That must have been the shiny object I saw when Dad put something in his drawer. At any rate, Melvin had taken out the clip that contained all of the bullets and placed it on the table. I was bored and wanted something to do also, so Jap let me finish cleaning the shotgun. He reminded us to hurry and finish and to put the guns up because our folks would be home in an hour or so. Jap went for a walk, while Melvin and I finished the guns.

I remember breaking open the chamber and looking down the long barrel of the shotgun. It was shiny and narrow in length and, I might add, it looked very creepy in there. I closed the shotgun and stood up to put it away, but as I got to the end of the dining room, Melvin had a sudden urge to play cowboys. We had played this game countless times, but never with real guns. He pointed the .45 at me and called my name. I turned around and obliged him by pretending to dodge his fire, and then I took aim at him as he did the same. As we circled for the final time, I was tired of playing, so I went into the bathroom to hide.

Melvin was persistent in continuing the game, as he tried to force the door open. I was unable to hold him at bay, for the simple reason that he was much stronger than I was. When he had gained force entry, I said, "Okay, I give up, don't shoot".

Melvin smiled and took a step backward, as if knowing this would give him the victory. I did not mind. I was just tired of playing and wanted to stop. After obtaining his distance, Melvin squared up, took aim, and fired. Only, instead of silence, the gun sounded like a cannon, knocking me backward and down on the floor. The gun expelled a sudden jolt when it fired, driving Melvin backward. He looked on in shock and disbelief at what had transpired. He knew the gun was not loaded, surely that was impossible.

Fear and uncertainty overwhelmed him immediately, as I lay there resembling a corpse. He began shaking and trembling uncontrollably, unable to hold back the terror and agony that gripped him. As my eyes slowly opened, I could vaguely see a figure standing in the hallway drop a shiny object, and then cover his face with his hands. I was dazed and unaware of what had transpired. I raised my eyelids and gazed above me. The underside of the toilet was staring me in the face. Everything was a blur, but I kept trying to focus my eyes.

Finally, my vision focused and the color of the walls indicated I was in the bathroom on the floor. Why was I in here and what on earth was that perpetual loud ringing sound in my ears? I kept asking the noise to please stop, but it would not. I could not make sense of anything, nor the ringing noise and Melvin standing in the hallway, shaking and looking dazed. Finally I thought, *if I get up, the noise would go away.*

I slowly rose to my feet, but the noise continued, and I called out, "Melvin, what happened?" I could not hear myself speaking because the noise was very loud and persistent. It persisted until I could not stand it any longer. I became impatient and wanted some answers, so I began to cry. I ran to the front door, holding my head with both hands, trying to suppress the noise. I stood on the front porch crying, and suddenly I felt a sticky substance running down my face. I lowered my right hand to examine it; filled with blood, so much blood. I immediately panicked and went into shock.

I started screaming at the top of my lungs, "Jap, Miss Fernando, Jap, Miss Fernando, Jap, Miss Fernando"; I was crying hysterically and calling out their names with repetition. Miss Fernando was a neighbor across the street, who had always lent a loving hand, especially helping Mother when we were very small. She would come over some mornings and cook breakfast, wash clothes, and even help clean the house. She was a very loving person, who gave of herself totally, and lived a full and fruitful life of ninety-six years.

Some of the neighbors heard the gunshot. I guess they thought it had been a blowout or something. By this time, Jap was turning the corner and immediately recognized my voice screaming and yelling. He ran as fast as he could in an attempt to calm me down and to find out what had happened.

He sputtered, "Andy, what happened?"

I cried, "Jap, Melvin shot me with Daddy's gun." Jap quickly picked me up, carried me across the street, and laid me down on the grass in a neighbor's yard. I was partially in the shade, but the side that was bleeding was collecting radiation from the scorching hot sun. In all the excitement, no one thought of moving me completely into the shade or shielding me from the sun's penetrating rays. *Come to think of it*, most of them probably were afraid to move me.

I remember the neighbors gathering, neighbors who had in some cases, never spoken to each other or had stopped speaking for some reason or another. People were yelling, "Call the ambulance, get a cool towel, don't move him", and so on. I even remember two of the neighbors arguing over which hospital to send me.

McLendon Hospital was right around the corner from us, but their facilities were limited. On the other hand, Grady Memorial Hospital, which at the time was the largest hospital in Atlanta, had all the facilities necessary for a gunshot trauma. Nevertheless, it was a "catch twenty-two" situation. If they took me to McLendon and the necessary equipment was not available, I might die during that time. On the other hand, Grady Memorial was the ideal hospital, but there was a fear that I might die on the way, since it was ten miles away.

During the excitement, Jap went back to the house to get Melvin and to call the police, because a report needed filing. The neighbors succeeded in contacting my mother at her job and one of them went to meet her at the bus stop. Melvin was still in shock and needed reassurance that everything would be all right. Jap took him to the Fernando's home, where he began pacing up and down the floor, praying that this was just a terrible nightmare. He thought he would never awaken from what seem like a dreadful and terrifying figment of the imagination because it was extremely realistic and full of pain and sorrow. Despite our differences, Melvin and I loved one another, and we played together quite often. He was more of a homebody than Jap. I looked to Jap for security because he always did the best things in the time of a crisis, and he was very energetic, the same as I was.

The ambulance from Grady somehow arrived before McLendon. I did not realize it then, but I know now that providence had taken over and it was an act of God intervening. The medics quickly removed their cot and placed me on it, after bandaging my head and checking my blood pressure. I intermittently slip in and out of consciousness, and overheard one of the medics say, "He is losing too much blood. We *gotta* work fast." As they finished and were in the process of placing me in the ambulance, my mother arrived. She explained who she was, and they allowed her to ride with me. Approximately fifty or sixty people had gathered during this tragic and very emotional accident, which left a dreadful memory engraved in the hearts and minds of viewers and our neighbors.

The ambulance driver was very skilled in his profession; he bobbed and weaved through traffic and wasted no time getting to the expressway. I regained consciousness and found myself in a state of serene peace, seeing my mother by my side holding my hand.

I uttered, "Hi Mommie".

She looked at me with deep motherly concern and responded, "Hi Sweetheart. You must not talk. Save all of your strength. Mommie will be right here". That was all I needed to hear, so I closed my eyes for a mere second. When I opened them, I was in a room lying on a table and no one was in the room with me. A few minutes later, my mother came after giving Admissions the information they required.

She walked over to me and said, "Anthony, how are you feeling?"

I replied, "Mommie, I feel okay". I did not want her to know that I was beginning to hurt badly. Suddenly, I said, "Mommie am I going to die? Please don't let me die." My mother had always had a strong faith in God, and through her persevering faith in Jesus Christ, we had made it through some difficult times. The question now was could we make it through this agonizing crisis? The doctor told her that if I lived, I would be nothing more than a vegetable.

Mother looked at me with an honest expression and remarked, "Anthony, do you remember when you lost your front teeth, and it seemed as though they would never grow back? I told you, if you showed faith in Jesus and prayed for them to grow back, that they would. Well, now you have to call on that same faith and that same Jesus because He is the only One who can sustain life."

While I listened to Mother's inspiring words, I was unaware of the prognosis the doctor gave her. His examination revealed I had lost a tremendous amount of blood, which had passed the critical stage. He further stated that my physical status was extremely weak and my chances of survival during surgery were very slim. In conclusion, he surmised, I did not have long to live and it was just a matter of time before the death angel arrived.

Mother and I prayed together, and now that I look back, I can honestly say I have never prayed so hard and earnestly in my life. An hour went by, and the doctor came in and examined me again. Astonished due to my sustaining pulse; he abruptly decided to scrub and operate. I remember an attendant wheeled me into a room that was ice cold, but all I could do was lie quietly and freeze. I vaguely remember the details that occurred in the operating room, although I do recall nurses wheeling in surgical instruments and other technical equipment. Someone placed a nozzle with a hose extension over my mouth and nose, which allowed me to breathe ether, an anesthetic that caused me to fall into a deep sleep.

While I was unconscious, I dreamt I was being stuck with all types of needles and cut in various places. I thought the torture would never end, until I heard someone say, "Anthony, would you like some apple juice?" It was my mother, who had spent the night at the hospital. My father was also there, but I was unaware of it at the time.

A man dressed in a plain dark suit came into the room and spoke with my mother and father. He was a detective in charge of the case. My parents gave him permission to ask me some questions. I was experiencing a severe amount of pain, and it increased as I spoke with him. He made it short and simple. He inquired if my brother shot me and if it was an accident. I answered yes to both questions, and he proceeded to leave. Periodically, throughout the night, I slept quietly and very still. It seemed as though every time I managed to get comfortable, a nurse would come in to give me a shot or some medicine. They were in and out constantly attending to me. They gave me plenty of juices, which assisted in bringing my temperature down, and helped rebuild my blood. Although annoying, I must admit that I received the best of care from all of the attending nurses.

The next day I continued to drift in and out of consciousness. The nurses came in during one of my stage of consciousness and informed me that some special people had come to see me. From nowhere, appeared two men with sunglasses. They were the star celebrities on the weekend series, "The Whirly Birds". They were in town visiting the different hospitals and cheering up many sick people with their presence. I cannot explain what their visit did for me. Although I was barely conscious, I still remembered extending my hand to shake theirs, and that gave me a solemn feeling of gratitude. I will never forget that feeling as long as I live. May God's blessings rest upon them and others that selflessly give of themselves to the sick and others that need love and a kind gesture. Coincidentally, "The Lone Ranger" was also in town visiting various elementary schools. Unfortunately, I missed seeing him, but I was grateful for the opportunity I did have to meet "The Whirly Birds".

As the following week approached, I slowly regained total

consciousness. I finally came to grips with the fact that the ceiling light, which was staring me in the face each morning was not the same one in my bedroom, but I was in the hospital. Visitors had come and gone, most of whom I was not even aware. All of them played a part in assisting in my recovery. Scores of get-well cards had come, but not opened for quite some time, eventually the right time would present itself. The doctors were unable to explain my amazing improvement. However, I knew that God bestowed in me an inner desire to live, coupled with the prayers of family and friends that played an important part in my miraculous recovery.

The early morning sunlight filtered slowly into the room as Mom pulled back the curtains and opened the blinds. I asked Mom to raise my bed for the first time. I felt more alive this day than in all the days that I spent so far in the hospital. As we began talking, a compulsion to scratch the right side of my face, which I could not resist, overwhelmed me. I could scarcely relieve the itch due to the bandage, which I soon found out wrapped my entire head and one-fourth of my face. What had appeared as obscure fragments suddenly crystallized for the first time since my hospitalization. Flashbacks began triggering portions of the traumatic accident. In what seemed like only seconds, I began piecing everything together.

Mom suddenly felt powerless, caught *between a rock and a hard place*. Reluctant to say anything, for fear that it would set ablaze the spark that began to ignite. To everyone's chagrin, it was too late; the spark burst forth into raging flames.

I screamed, "Oh my God! My eye, my eye Mommie, where is my eye? I don't want to lose my eye", I continued to cry, although Mom attempted to comfort me.

"Don't cry, sweetheart. Everything is going to be okay. Just put your trust in God's hand," she said.

However, words of comfort could not penetrate deep enough to ease the pain I experienced. I cried until I fell asleep, hoping this nightmare was just a dream. Unfortunately, I later awakened with the same painful memory and its evidence. Only this time, I was able to discuss it rationally with my mother without bursting into tears. She expressed various reasons why I should be thankful.

Mother said, "Anthony, God's sovereign will was to spare your life, and He has blessed you to have sight in one eye. Think about how blessed you are to be alive and healthy." The things she conveyed enabled me to see my handicap from a new perspective, yet deep inside I felt my life would never be the same.

Subsequently, things did change for me. I was aware of the things around me more, and I was emotionally sensitive to a greater degree than in the past. Feelings surfaced that I was oblivious to previously or had failed to consider. It took me a considerable amount of time to adjust to these new and awkward feelings.

As time passed, I learned to cope not only with my present state of emotions, but also to respond to them in a healthy manner. I acquired, through self-determination, the ability to overcome any feelings of inadequacy and sensitivity. I was unaware, but I later discovered that I had cast an image of total "self-confidence", instead of "Christ-Confidence". As for my self-confidence, it appeared to aid me considerably in the development of my self-image. Only time would reveal the effects and outcome of my experiencing what seemed to me a tragedy.

Aftermath: Marred by Accidental Violence

Chapter Four

NIGHTMARES

✻ ✻ ✻

TEACHER'S PET

The hospital staff advised us of my discharge date in the following two weeks. I did not know whether I was happy or sad, since I had made many friends. I felt rather protected in the hospital, never having to worry about being different or feeling like an outcast. I knew there were times when people appeared cruel, cold, and uncaring. On the other hand, I missed being home with family. I knew I could depend on them for strong support, for we had always had a strong family tie.

Friends and relatives continued to visit me, and I enjoyed them. But, the strangest thing was that if anyone was there when my father arrived, I would escort them to the door and sometimes down the hall, so I could have him to myself. I cannot understand, to this day, why I did that, because he was no more than your average father was. I can honestly say it brought pure joy to my heart, beyond imagination, whenever my dad entered the room. What a mystery!

The doctor gave me a final examination one day and released me. Mom purchased some new clothes for me to wear home. The clothes brightened my spirits, somewhat, but nothing could divert my attention from my fear and self-consciousness. I felt safe as long as the black patch was covering the eye area, but even that drew some attention. Mother escorted me to the elevator in a wheelchair, hospital rules, of course. A cab was waiting downstairs to drive us home. Time looked as though it had stood still. Everything looked the same, and downtown Atlanta was as busy as always.

We arrived home while the boys were still in school. I had a bite to eat and watched television for a while. At three-thirty, I heard a key unlocking the front door. It was Jap and Melvin arriving home at the same time. I was a bit nervous. Why, I cannot explain, even though they had recently been to see me in the hospital. Jap spotted me a few seconds before Melvin but it seemed as though they both broke out in spontaneous joy after discovering my arrival. They acted as if they had not seen me in ages and began introducing me to some of their new toys. Before you knew it, the nervousness passed and it was as if I had not been away at all. Some of the neighbors found out I was out of the hospital and dropped by with warm greetings, which made me feel even better.

Soon after my confidence improved, I was able to go and visit other neighbors. The prosthesis, which my mother purchased for me, had a lot to do with the improvement in my self-esteem. It was not the best, but it was what our money could afford. This made my thoughts of returning to school more bearable. The nightmares I had experienced, relating to my first day back to school, were not pretty pictures by a long shot. In one of my dreams, everyone stood around me making fun of my handicap. In another dream, the teacher asked me to come to the front of the class and remove my patch so everyone could relieve their curiosity, only at my expense. Boy was I thankful to awaken and find out that these were only nightmares.

I was in somewhat of a good mood and decided to do some reading. I thought, "what better time to read all the get-well cards is there than now?" My state of being was sound, which enabled me to get in touch with each card or person emotionally. The get-well cards generated affirmative feelings of warm sentiment, and I was happy that I had wanted to read them. I was particularly grateful for the card and letter that Terrie sent me. Her letter indicated she was deeply sorry about my misfortune and if I needed her to do anything, she was just a phone call away. I decided to keep and treasure her letter forever, but somehow it got lost in the shuffle.

My best friend, Reginald Love, kept in touch with me and alerted me to the fact that Terrie would soon be transferring to the Collier Drive Elementary School. I was very saddened by the news, not knowing if I would ever see her again, but the hands of time continued forward and so did my life.

It was my first day back at school after the accident. I had been out about two months, and believe me, they were the longest two months of my life. My classmates were nothing as I had imagined them to be in the scenarios of my dreams. Everyone was generous and kind to me, and tried to please me in any way possible. My teacher had discussed make-up tests with my mother, which would bring me up to date with the rest of the class. I studied very hard, took the necessary tests, and passed them all. I was glad I had passed the tests, but I became very worried when I noticed my grade point average had dropped from 3.8 to 2.5.

My mother was alarmed also, and discussed with the doctor our concerns. He admitted that there was an expectation to some degree of a decline in my IQ, but whether or not I would regain my total learning potential was hard to say. He explained to her, that during the course of the operation, bullet fragments were found in the brain area. Although, there was no visible damage found, he still could not guarantee if there were no other injuries or impairments to the brain. The bottom line was that only time would tell whether I would fully recover from the setback. Before things got worse, they took a turn for the better. Since I was aware of my setback, I realized it was entirely up to me to make every effort to improve grades. Therefore, I made up my mind to study harder.

There were other problems resulting from this potential damage. I noticed a loss of hearing in the right ear, but it was not enough to cause concern. I also developed a nervous condition, which resulted in me biting my nails and a stutter in speech. It was most difficult adjusting to these disabilities at the same time. It took a great deal of patience and hard work to overcome them, which enabled me to function like a normal human being. No longer did I take my ears for granted. I used ear protection whenever warranted, and in about twelve years, my hearing improved immensely.

I fought a six-year battle with my nail biting habit, and it got to the point where I bit clear down to the cuticle. After six years, the desire had exhausted itself and dissipated, just as it had appeared. I did not completely resolve my stammering, although through practice, time, and patience, I learned to control it, and not let it control me.

I passed the fourth grade with no problems academically, but there was that same emotional problem I had to deal with in the third grade. Every year, all students were required to take an eye test to judge their sight ability.

I did not mind doing the eye test, but what I did object, was standing before the entire class during the test. I cannot express what an emotional strain this ordeal placed on me. I worried about that test far more than any other test, and it would linger on my mind months before it was scheduled. I sincerely feel that if I were a teacher, during that time, and knew of my student's traumatic experience, my protective instincts as a teacher for my student would kick in on his or her behalf. I would take into account their emotional stability during that time.

Mrs. Stanley, my fifth-grade teacher, was a fine example of the type of teacher I had hoped to have. She was a young and pretty woman, who displayed a genuine interest in all of her students. She made you feel free to come and talk to her about any problem or difficulty you were experiencing. To her, stupid questions were the ones that people often wanted to ask, however were too afraid to ask. She was a very sweet and terrific person that I had the pleasure of being one of her students. She was fond of me, and others made remarks, saying that I was the teacher's pet. You may or may not find some truth in those statements, but I do know that I liked Mrs. Stanley better than I did any of my other teachers. I thought about her quite often, as if I was experiencing my second boyhood crush.

I would arrive to school early each morning, just to sit and talk with her before class began. We talked about my family, her family, and her vacation plans for Christmas, which was not far away. Other students eventually became aware of my early arrival and made it their business to do the same. This made me angry, to say the least. I felt like this was an invasion of privacy. But, what gave me the exclusive right to have her all to myself? After all, she was their teacher too. After thinking things through, God gave me a change of heart and I decided to share that time with whomever.

School was out for Christmas and the holidays that followed. Everyone went his or her separate way to help spread the Christmas cheer. Mrs. Stanley and her family left town to visit relatives. My family decided to spend the holidays with my aunt Irene, who was my mother's sister and she had just purchased a lovely home. Christmas was sure to be in top form this year because the weatherman had predicted a white Christmas and hit it right on the button. We had an enjoyable time exchanging gifts and giving thanks to our Lord for the blessings we had received.

It was approaching New Year's Eve, and we all gathered in my aunt's den, listening to the news. The news anchor gave a death count of the people who died thus far, over the holidays. He spoke of one tragedy, whereby a family was traveling toward Atlanta, when two drunken teenagers headed in the opposite direction collided with them. The teenage driver lost control of his car, causing it to plow head-on with the oncoming car at a high rate of speed. The force of the impact threw their bodies out of the car, causing broken and dislocated bone injuries. The wife's body ejected from the car through the windshield separating it beyond recognition. The news anchor reported that she was a schoolteacher at Frank L. Stanton Elementary and her name was Mrs. Stanley.

My mouth fell open in shock and disbelief, while my eyes became full of tears. I kept refusing to believe what I had heard, but the bottom line was that I knew it was true. Two days later, I went to view the body for myself and looked reality in the face. I cried, oh, how I cried, and afterward said a prayer in her behalf. However, it was difficult for me to come to grips with how senseless her death appeared. Other classmates visited the body also, while some paid their respects to the family.

For the rest of the school term, Miss Beasley was Mrs. Stanley's appointed replacement. She was okay, but there would never be another to take the place of Mrs. Stanley. Many of the students liked Miss Beasley because she often gave us extra recess time. Sometimes, we were outdoors playing and she along with some of the others teachers had intensive conversations that lasted so long that they allowed us to stay out an extra thirty minutes. I remember one day, Miss Beasley allowed us to stay out for two hours. We played all nine innings of a baseball game. Boy was that some game!

One of the guys in my class, Carl Boxstale purchased several oatmeal cookies for lunch every day. Each day, I probed and prodded him for one and assured him I would repay him. Well, by the time I had consumed about twenty of his cookies and had not given him anything in return, the air got a little thick.

He asked me to pay him for the cookies, and I immediately said, "Okay, Carl, I'll bring your money tomorrow." Somehow, tomorrow turned into a week and I still had not paid him. Maybe, it was because I did not take him seriously or something. After school one day, I was alone because I decided to stop and talk with Reginald for about thirty minutes; the other kids headed for home right after school. The traffic gradually began increasing. The beginning of the five o'clock rush hour was nearly underway. I always walked home on the left side of the street. For some reason or another, I felt safer on that side.

But, today, that side turned out to be the unlucky side, for as I turned the corner, Carl and his older brother approached me from the opposite direction. It was too late for me to run or hide, for it would have been too obvious, so I marched solemnly right into their arms. They were at least three or four inches taller than I was, and that made the situation just that much more threatening.

We met face to face, as they blocked my passage, and the older brother said, "My brother tells me you owe him some money, punk. Well, you'd better pay up in full right now." I looked a little glassy-eyed, as well as stunned, for fear became rooted deep within me. However, through it all, I tried to remain cool as I replied, "Okay, man, I'll pay up. Let's see, I have some money in one of these pockets."

During my bogus search for money, I diverted their attention. I broke through them suddenly without warning. I had always been one of the fastest runners in my school, and now was the time for me to live up to that reputation.

I ran low, hard, and fast, but to no avail. There was only a little distance between us. I had a tear in my right shoe in the rear, and it threatened to fall off any second. Sure enough, it fell off, but the guys were too close for me to stop and pick it up, so I ran without that shoe. A lady stood at the bus stop, ready to board the approaching bus, I ran up to her and shouted, "Ma'am will you tell those boys to leave me alone?" The Boxstale brothers stood at the bus stop in anticipation of making the attack, as the lady tried to decide what to say. The bus stopped, the door opened, and the lady said, "You boys go on home and behave yourselves". She boarded the bus and the bus driver pulled off. The brothers looked at me with blood in their eyes, and the chase resumed from where it had left off.

Luckily, I was only three blocks away from home because we ran the total distance. Just when I was almost ready to collapse from exhaustion and fear, I made it to my yard.

I ran into the house where Melvin and my mother were sitting down talking. I entered the room, and Mother looked up and said, "Anthony, why are you huffing and puffing?"

I bent over to catch my breath and to ease the cramping pains in my stomach. Then, I replied in tears, "Some boys were chasing me". After making that statement, I cried heavily, in a sigh of relief after escaping the two brothers. Mother wanted to know why they were chasing me, plus all the other details. Stating my case only put me in hotter water with Mom. She made me apologize and give the boy his money for the cookies. I was extremely embarrassed, but glad that it was over; Melvin went with me to the place where my shoe had come off. We retrieved my shoe, and the story had a somewhat of a happy- ending. I learned a valuable lesson I would never forget.

High School Adolescent Years

Chapter Five

NEW CLASSMATE

Summer went by very swiftly, and it was time to begin school all over again. I had been talking to an old friend of mine who lived around the corner in my neighborhood, and he was considering a transfer to my school. I did everything I could to encourage him to make the move. He made his debut with me the first day of school and introduced himself as Tony Ross. I showed him around and introduced him to some of the guys.

Inside of a month, Tony had everybody eating out of his hand, and that included the girls. I felt as though he had moved in on my territory and staked his claim. Everyone simply adored him and I became jealous. Even though, he appeared to be a little naïve and innocent, underneath, I knew he was aware of what he was doing. He had all of my followers captivated by his charisma. After school, the guys would flock to his house or on his street to be around him. His parents bought him a go-cart for Christmas, and the fellows went completely "off". It seemed as though there was some kind of magnetic energy urging everybody to go to his house.

I know how I may sound to some of you, but if only you could have been there, it was a sight to see. I too, was guilty of visiting him too much. When I realized what was happening I made an adjustment in my habits. Tony remained unaware of the tension that developed between us and still looked to me as his best friend. Not many knew it, but there were other times when he really gave me a pain in the neck, if you know what I mean.

How many of you ever had a friend who tried to talk to every girl that you had a crush. Well, I had a first-hand experience like that with this character and I did not like it one bit. I had my eyes on a girl named Gail. I asked her for a chance one morning before class, and she decided to let me know the following day. During this time, my dear friend, Tony got wind of what had transpired so he decided to ask her for one also. The next morning I came in bright-eyed and bushy-tailed expecting to receive some good news only to receive a slap in the face.

I was sitting in the classroom telling a friend about the good news that might be developing that morning, when in walked Tony with the look of love on his face. Tony took a seat next to a girl named Marie, who said, "OOO Wee, Tony, Gail told me you asked her to go steady."

Tony boastfully replied, "So."

Marie appeared astonished by his reply and rebutted, "So, you could have asked me first, but that's all right, go on with your bad self".

By this time, I was ready to boil over with anger, coupled with embarrassment. If Gail had said yes to Tony, I would certainly feel like a complete fool in the mirror. As Tony came over and took a seat, I laid my head down on my desk.

He greeted James and me, and I just nodded while James asked him a question: "Hey, little Tony, did you really ask Gail for a chance?"

Tony smiled and casually said, "Yeah, man, I just jokingly phoned her and asked her. But, you know what? It shocked me when she took me seriously and said yes. Man, I freaked out, but of course, she did not know it. Hey James, what is the matter with Anthony? Is he sick or something?"

James remarked, "I think he said his stomach was hurting." My stomach was hurting all right. But, this pain did not result from something that I ate. I ached from the pain responding to the anger that shot sporadically through my body. I cannot forget how furious it made me when Tony said that he was just joking with Gail, and all the while, I was dead serious about her.

I remained angry for some time, although Tony was not any wiser. One day, while thumbing through my notebook, looking for a clean sheet of paper, I stumbled upon a letter from Gail. She explained her reason for not being able to grant my request. The reason was that someone else asked her before she responded to me. Her letter stated that maybe I would get a chance with her in the distant future, I did not know whether to believe her or not. All I knew was that there had to be some rational type of explanation to make some sense out of the scenario. Here again, I chalked it all up to experience. The letter did not erase the pain and hurt that I had experienced, but it enabled me to put things into a better perspective.

In the meantime, life went on and with it came new distractions, which were most appealing to the eye. A set of twin boys, along with their sister joined our class at mid-semester. Known as the Thornton twins and, I might add, they were a handsome pair in their own right. Their sister, Claudine was draped in natural beauty, with a figure that any guy would find pleasing to the eye. She generally wore her hair loose and carefree. One might say she seemed to enjoy the attention she received from her onlookers, as her lovely hair dangled below her waist.

You could have carved these three out of a storybook because they fitted the bill perfectly. They were extremely nice and well mannered, and the whole school thought a lot of them. It goes without saying they will forever have a place in the hearts of my sixth and seventh-grade class. The Thorntons hosted several parties at their home, and we all had a great time. They had two of the most warm-hearted parents I had ever met. Whenever they invited us to their home, we received the red carpet treatment. Oh, well, so much for a stroll down Memory Lane.

Mr. Cleveland was our seventh-grade teacher and our first male instructor. He was a nice person and rather timid. It was his belief that the more homework a person had, the more he or she would learn. That explained why he piled the work on us big time. My task was to pass the science books out each day and someone else collected them at the end of the class.

On this particular day, it was about one-fifteen in the afternoon and I had bent over in the cabinet to get the books when another teacher came into the room rolling a television set. At first, we thought it was a science program that she wanted us to see, but we found out different when she turned on the news with a breaking broadcast. Everybody was curious when we saw the new bulletin flash on the screen. The reporter announced that President John F. Kennedy had just been shot. The terrible news caused mourning to run rampant across the room. Shock and dismay was apparent on all of our faces as we gazed at the television, and I remember experiencing a harsh pain in my chest. It was the same feeling I felt when my schoolteacher died.

Later, the reporter stated that an assassin's bullet shot and killed the president. Eventually there was an arrest of the accused assassin, Lee Harvey Oswald, later gunned down while transferring him through an underground police department's garage; but, not prior to this horrific criminal act taking the nation by storm. Vice President Lyndon B. Johnson assumed the office of the presidency. America's resilience allowed her to bounce back in an effort to live out her true heritage.

Months passed and it was time for graduation. Parties along with our sweethearts' ball were all unforgettable, but none of these occasions could erase the fact that a lot of us would be going separate ways. My graduation, filled with tears of despair in recognition of the good times we shared knowing that we would probably share them no more.

The eighth grade was a drastic change in my academic career, because Washington High School discontinued its eighth grade and made it mandatory that everybody transfer to Central Junior High, a school located downtown Atlanta. So, there I was, in an unknown school with unknown teachers and quite a few unknown students. However, over a period of time, I managed to make the transition, and things eventually began to flow in a normal pattern, I even began to enjoy and look forward to everyday activities that we experienced in each class.

I later discovered that one of my neighbors taught in the Science Department, and I might add that his looks far more intrigued the young ladies than his teaching ability. Although Mr. Carl Fouch was a wizard at his craft, there were times when he seemed to be more or less a workaholic. He would pile homework on us as if there was no tomorrow. Yet somehow or another, we all liked him.

My coach, Mr. Hogan, had a great deal of influence on his students. He had a muscular physique along with a warm but firm personality to match. We did exercise every morning and boy, did we ever exercise! As I reminisce, I do believe the whole school attempted to advocate a new awakening in the physical fitness realm. But, as time rolled on, we began to enjoy the workouts, and the volleyball games, even though our team seldom won.

Our attention remained focused on the fun we were having and before we knew it, the year had taken flight and was gone. Moreover, with it went the new familiarities we shared, the fun, and the endless laughter, which we will never forget. In addition, standing in the wings waiting patiently for me, just as Mother Nature silently waits for her spring flowers to bloom was another new and unknown experience setting its stage at Booker T. Washington High School. Fear of the unknown always plagued my emotions, but somehow I would always persevere and rise above it all.

Chapter Six

ADOLESCENT FEARS

My church habits, at this point, were very *few and far between*, which made me solely ripe and ready for the things of this world. Even though, I experienced somewhat of a religious upbringing. From time to time, it still was not consistent enough in my life to ward off the temptations of Satan. Women began to surface on my mind more and more, while I listened to the sound of Major Lance, Jackie Wilson, Elvis Presley, and the Temptations. I always sang around the house a lot as a child, and my brothers teased me, saying that I had an operatic type voice. Their mocking did not bother me because I loved to sing and always felt compelled to do so.

On the first day at Booker T. Washington High School, I found myself a little apprehensive and a bit afraid, or to be even more candid, I should admit that it felt terrifying to me. Booker T as most students referred to our school had a reputation of being a very tough school and lived up to every bit of it. Our principal, J. Y. Moreland believed that strong leadership is the backbone to becoming successful, so he practiced his ethics on us.

I registered for ROTC as one of my elective classes. I discovered from a movie on television that a woman likes a man in uniform and thought I would try my luck. My given assignment was the A Company, First Platoon, and the Third Squad. My platoon leader was an arrogant, self-centered individual who rode a person's back whenever he felt the need to assert himself. I did my best to stay within his good graces. One of the squad cadets, Dwight Franklin received a lot of ridicule and hardship from him. Subsequently, Dwight became a close friend of mine.

We left school early one day and went over to his house to listen to the Temptations' *Mellow Mood* album. I had an enjoyable time that day, although my ears were not accustomed to music played and *turned up* to such a high volume. Our friendship grew closer as we started meeting and singing in the bathroom after classes each day.

I clearly remember the day we met Ricky Bellows; it was approximately a week after the Temptations' *I Wish It Would Rain* album debut. Rick came into the restroom and we stopped singing. To our amazement, it was too late; he overheard us singing before entering the restroom. Normally, we heard a person before they entered the restroom and would immediately stop singing before the door opened; however, in this case, our timing was off.

Ricky introduced himself and asked us if he could harmonize with us. Dwight nodded and we began singing *Grooving*. He had a beautiful voice, which was a natural second tenor. Dwight and I looked at each other in astonishment, as we continued singing. The harmony sounded so good that we failed to notice the other guys gathering in the restroom. They began putting their books on the floor and leaning up against the walls. We finished *Grooving* and then we inquired if he knew the lead part to *I Wish It Would Rain* that had only been on the market for roughly a month. Ricky nodded yes, he knew it, and without a hint of shyness, he started to sing. We were stunned how close he came to sounding like the record. The only difference in his voice was that it was soft and mellow, and the singer's voice on the record sounded tough and rough, and full of years of experience.

We decided to call it quits after about an hour. One of the guys asked if we were a group, and we immediately said, "No".

He told us how good we sounded and that it might not be a bad idea to start one. I went home that day thinking of all the pros and cons of forming a group and the demands it would bring. I was a basketball fanatic and played at the neighborhood playground every day after school. Now at this part of my life, basketball was the priority, and that meant even before the girls. Therefore, at the thought of singing interfering with my game, suddenly it *turned me off* at the idea of forming a group.

The next day at school, Dwight and I were walking down the hall together and two guys passed us singing. *What's Your Name* and their harmony was unbelievable, but somehow or another, we lost them in the crowd. That afternoon, Dwight and I met in the restroom as usual, and lo and behold, the two who were harmonizing earlier were there too. They were singing *The Duke of Earl* and with the acoustics of the restroom, it caused the sound to bounce off the walls. Their voices projected a sound as if there were four or five of them singing together. They asked us to join them. I guess, one way or another, they had heard that we could sing also. We blended our harmony with theirs and before we knew it, the restroom became jam-packed with onlookers. Later, I learned their names were Eric Daniel and Seal Carr.

We practiced for thirty minutes, and Dwight mentioned the idea of forming a group because there was a *Future Family of America* talent show about two months away. We made little or no conversation about it, so all dispersed and headed for home. I slowly walked home that day thinking about what transpired when I heard footsteps behind me. I glanced around and was literally stunned at the beauty of the young lady behind me. I decided to wait for her and I kept repeatedly thinking, *Wow, she is the most beautiful girl I have ever seen, that is, beside Terrie.*

I greeted her as she walked up to me. "Hello, my name is Anthony, and yours?"

Her voice was sweet and innocent as she replied, "My name is Jean Horton". I responded, "Well Jean, it is most definitely a pleasure to meet you, and might I add, you are a very attractive young lady". She thanked me for the polite comment and left the door open for further conversation. She was on her way to visit her grandmother, who lived approximately three blocks from me. I insisted on walking with her and she graciously accepted. I knew the answer to my next question before I even asked it, but I wanted to hear it from her lips.

I said, "Are you dating anyone at the present time?"

"No, I am usually busy with my studies and all with not

much time for other things". I felt like someone hit me in the head with a golf ball when she answered my question. Never in a million years would I imagine that she was available. I concluded that this must be my lucky day, and if I was on a roll, then why not continue. My fingers on my right hand started shaking as I braced myself to ask my next question.

"Well, do you mind if I call you sometimes?"

"Of course not at all, as a matter of fact, you can call me at my grandmother's tonight. I am spending the weekend with her," she replied. Boy, people talk about batting a thousand. Well, right about then, I felt like I was *Hammerin' Hank (Aaron)* who had hit his 715th home run.

I called Jean and we talked for a while. I found that she had a twin sister and they attended Booker T. Washington. Her sister's name was Virginia and although they were not identical, Virginia was pretty also and had a beautiful personality. After about two weeks, Jean and I started dating.

Atlanta Parliaments
L – R: Seal Carr, Eric Daniel, Ricky Bellows, Anthony Freeman, Dwight Franklin

Chapter Seven

GROWTH IN SELF-ESTEEM

❋❋❋

I was out playing ball one afternoon when I saw some familiar faces enter onto the playground. You guessed it, it was Dwight, Ricky, Eric and Seal. I must admit I was not particularly overjoyed to see them, especially during my basketball period. This was an unusual day and it sticks out in the back of my mind like a sore thumb, the day that I gave in to singing.

We walked back to my house and had a business meeting. We first organized the group, selected a president, a business manager, and a treasurer. We scheduled practice days from the calendar to prepare us for the upcoming talent show. The more days we scheduled for practice, the less time I had to spend with Jean. However strange as it seem this character trait was one that I had yet to comprehend. When it came down to business, I made a point to everyone that I meant strictly business and kept everything in its proper place and time. The way I had things figured out was that singing came first, basketball came second, and the women came during the time left. At first, it seemed as though Jean understood, at least it appeared that way. She thought this was a temporary *fly-by-night* singing group. What she did not realize was that she had to compete with it all year long.

Occasionally, I went to the YMCA on Thursday nights to a dance, by myself, of course. On this particular night, as I left, I noticed a crowd gathering around the television. At first glance, I thought they were watching a special football game or something. As I paid closer attention, I realized it was no game, but that it was a special broadcast announcing the death of Dr. Martin Luther King, Jr. Oh, the sudden agony plagued my heart at that very moment. A man who had given his all to humanity, a man who fought against the injustices of the system, a man who fed the hungry and clothed the naked, now shot and killed by an assassin's bullet.

Anger and rage raced across the streets of Atlanta, Detroit, Memphis, Chicago, et cetera. People were burning, rioting, and looting in protest against violence. Mrs. King vowed, they may have killed the man, but her husband's dream would never die. To insure that it did not, she would not rest until the birthday of Dr. Martin Luther King, Jr. was recognized and treated as a national holiday. As a result, this inspired other Americans to push toward making his dream a reality.

Time had run out, and it was time for the *Future Family of America* talent show. Groups had come out of the wood-works to make an appearance on this show. The show's musicians whom they hired were seemingly professional and did not complain at all about the many groups that needed to rehearse with them. We decided to call ourselves *The Parliaments that* sounded a lot better than the name we had been given in the restroom at school. Better known as *The Toileteers,* it was a name given us by a smart-aleck student. We met a band named *The Upsetters* who were much older than we were and who had a very good sound. We decided to use them on the talent show.

We learned the entire *Mellow Mood* album plus the entire *Temptation Live* album, and we now thought of ourselves as ripe and ready. Our key song entitled *Losing You*, was a very powerful song at the time, so I took the lead on that one. We worked up some real sharp choreography to most of our songs, and that is the reason why practicing was time-consuming. After learning each song, we then had to choreograph a step routine, and believe me, that took considerable time.

We met a young lady at one of the rehearsals who asked if we would sing background to her song on the talent show. Her name was Debra Davis; she was going to sing *Gladys Knight and the Pips', I Heard It through the Grapevine* release. We invited her over to practice with us. By this time, word was out that Motown had put together a memorial for the late Dr. Martin Luther King, Jr., and it was to take place on the same night as the talent show. Motown held the memorial at the Atlanta Civic Center, which was only a few blocks down from the Atlanta City Auditorium.

Jean waited faithfully in the wings through all of this, and somehow, no matter how late it was, I drove by her house on my way home and spent a few minutes with her. Each time, she became hot and angry with me, but then she soon cooled off and came to me in spite of it all. Our telephone conversations progressively grew cold as an ice cube. Sometimes, I thought that I was conversing with myself. As I look back now, I could not blame any woman for not wanting to play *second fiddle* to a man's career.

The stage was set, and the curtains were due to go up at eight o'clock. We rented tuxedos that afternoon and now began to get a small case of the jitters, but it soon passed. We realized that this was our first major debut, and we wanted so much to present ourselves as a well-polished group to our audience. There were said to be more than fifty acts on bill that night from different high schools, so we knew that we had more than our share of competition. Our group quickly became very close for such a brief time together, due to the back-to-back rehearsals that took place. Although, this would mark our first major debut, we previously had performances for a fashion tea and a small shower.

People began taking their seats early. Mothers, fathers, brothers, and sisters came out of the woodwork to support their contestants. The different groups were prompt and in place; they advised everyone beforehand that if each group performing were not there on time for the proper arrangement on program, they would substitute another contestant. There were cameras, tape recorders, and photographers all over the place. The turnout was more than we ever expected, since the Motown sound performed only a few blocks away. I guess it was a possibility that the tickets for their performance were too high for some people and they decided to come and hear some local talent. Well, we did not disappoint anyone because the talent that was on hand was some of the best in all Atlanta.

The curtains went up at approximately eight o'clock and the emcee walked to center stage and welcomed everyone to the *Future Family of America's* citywide talent show. He introduced the opening act, and they came out and did an instrumental number, which helped warm up the crowd. They scheduled our group as the seventh act to perform on program and that was just fine with us. We did not want our performance too early nor did we want to perform too late.

Programmed to perform on stage prior to our group was the girl group, the *Epics*, and when they came out, they literally brought the house down with a song by *Aretha Frank, titled Ain't No Way.* These girls had very mature and professional voices for their ages, and when the soprano displayed that she could hold her note longer than the record, the crowd really went wild. The girls left the stage receiving a standing ovation, the crowd begged for more, the girls made their exit, and it was our turn to try and prove ourselves worthy for the first-place prize. The curtains closed and the emcee announced a slight pause for intermission to allow our band to plug in their equipment. We knew deep in our hearts that their performance was a tough act to follow, but if we had to lose, we preferred it to be to a girl group than a male group.

The Atlanta Parliaments Grooving on a Sunday Afternoon

The curtains were back up within five minutes, and the crowd was still hungry for action. The emcee introduced us as *The Atlanta Parliaments.* We gathered behind the stage with our heads bowed in prayer. This became a regular custom of ours, and we always did it prior to our stage performances. We entered the stage and opened up with Debra's song, I *Heard It through the Grapevine.* The crowd really enjoyed our performance. Debra had a mature voice for her age, and honestly speaking, I felt that she held her own that night. I guess she felt her chances were better if she had some background singers.

After her song, she left the stage and the guys backed me up on *Grooving.* I could not imagine, for the life of me, what all the girls were screaming about during our performance; I had never experienced such a reaction like this before, except at the birth of the Beatles. However, they continued to scream during the entire song. I thought to myself, *surely, if they scream on this slow song, they probably would go absolutely mad on the next one.* Can you envision what happened?

I was not too far wrong, because when the band began playing *I'm Losing You,* we broke down into our routine, and they went plumb crazy. They were in and out of their seats, and dancing in the aisles through the whole song. As we danced off the stage, we knew from that day forward our theme song would always be *I'm Losing You.*

Well, the show continued into the evening, the other acts were good also, but the crowd had their fill of the action. The five judges sat in front of the stage; they made notations all night. Then, in the final hour, it was time for the first, second, and third place winner's announcement. The emcee came to the center stage with envelopes. The audience got very quiet and still. He announced that the third-place prize was fifty dollars, and Miss Debra Davis received the award. We hugged and kissed Debra as she cried with joy after accepting the prize.

This time the emcee asked for a drum roll as he announced the second-place winners of one hundred dollars were *The Atlanta Parliaments.* Dwight accepted the award for us; and boy, were we happy. Out of all the talented people who participated that night, we were grateful for any place available to us.

At last, the emcee asked for another drum roll and then announced that the first-place winners were the *Epics and they* received an award of one hundred and fifty dollars. The girls were overjoyed, and tears were everywhere. We were extremely happy for them, for they earned the right as the number one contestants. The audience clapped for them that stamped their approval of the judges' decision. Oh, what an unbelievable night it was for everyone. There were smiles, congratulations, hugs, and kisses, not to mention all the pats on the back for a job well done.

We left there on a mental, as well as an emotional high, as though we had conquered a nation or won a Grammy Award. The Dr. Martin Luther King Jr. benefit was still in progress when we got there, and with our having tuxedos on and dressed alike, the door attendant welcomed us. All eyes fell on us as we made our entrance. Instead of holding the benefit in the main auditorium, they held it in the room designated for presidential campaigns. I surmised that there were more than fifteen thousand people in that room, not to mention the scores of entertainers backstage.

**The Benefit Dr Martin Luther King Jr Brought
the Best Of the Best In Motown**

Let's see, *Stevie Wonder was there, Jr Walker and the All Stars, the Supremes, the Temptations, the Four Tops, Pattie LaBelle and the Blue Bells, Marvin Gaye, the Originals* and the list was not exhaustive. The *Motown Orchestra* played their hearts out as they brought on one act after another. People stared at us as we made our way backstage.

1-David Ruffin and Anthony Backstage Chatting 2 Anthony & Dr Feelgood

David Ruffin checked the crowd out from behind the curtains, and the other *Temps* touched up their makeup in their dressing room, but there were only four of them, instead of five. The *Supremes* draped in sparkling reddish-purple Egyptian styled costumes made them appear ancient and very petite.

There was so much happening at the same time that you did not know where to look next for fear that you would miss something. All the entertainers were great, and the benefit most definitely was a grand success. That night we went home with stars in our eyes and with the hope that some of that stardom would rub off on us somehow. I stopped by Jean's house and as usual, she was angry, so I did not stay long.

The group had to rise and shine early the next morning to go to the studio to take pictures, before returning the rented tuxedos. After having some professional shots done, we had copies run off and circulated them around town. In about a month's time, booking engagements started rolling in before we knew it. We did teas, fashion shows, nightclubs, and colleges. We made a lot of money performing for the colleges. Dwight handled most of the bookings, although every now and then, I booked us somewhere. It came to a point where bands enjoyed doing engagements with us, but we always protected the group and kept it separate. We did things that way for the simple reason that quite a few bands back then were a dime a dozen. They were here today and perhaps gone tomorrow, however, we knew we had a dependable group.

We worked during the day through the week and left the weekends open for engagements. Dwight and I worked for **St. Joe's Paper Company**, and Eric and Seal worked for **Mark Inn**. We set dates for the purchase of new uniforms and on those dates, we went downtown together and made the purchase. We even set a goal to buy a group car and a PA system, and it was a blessing for us that we were able to purchase both. Things moved right along. In fact, sometimes they move too fast.

One night Dwight booked a last-minute engagement and rounded up everybody, but me. He telephoned Jean at her home and she told him that I was not with her, but he knew I was with her all the time. The fellows left town and performed the engagement without me. I felt badly and knew then that I had let them down, but at the same time, I felt as though I owed that time to Jean.

About a month later, the same situation happened again and Jean thought I would allow her to deny my being with her, but this time I took the phone from her and told Dwight that I would come right away. Jean was hot *under the collar* and very upset with me, but then again so was I. I was not about to let myself get into that same situation again. I explained to her that I had to leave and that I would drop by to see her after our gig was over. She replied that if I walked out that door to forget about ever stopping by again to visit her. She gave me an ultimatum and I had to make a choice between her or the group.

That night, I understood the old saying, "*You can't have your cake and eat it too*". I drove away that night, never to return. Finally, I made a decision to stop dating and just become a loner. I could not give a woman the time she so desperately demanded. It was hard staying away from Jean, but I forced myself to do it, for the sake of the group. Things seem to go smoothly thus far and I did not want to rock the boat again.

It was graduation time for Dwight, Seal, and me. Eric was a year behind us and Ricky…well, Ricky was no longer with us. The group trimmed down to a foursome that required a little adjustment for us. Dwight booked two ROTC balls and two proms the previous year, so we were almost certain that we would book this year as well. We obtained the bookings to perform about a month later.

Chapter Eight

GROUP DEDICATION

✸ ✸ ✸

One night, we scheduled a rehearsal in Eric's basement and one of his sisters, Vicki whom I had never seen before was home. Although an attractive young lady, she appeared to look too young for me. It would not have made any difference to me because up to this point I was firm about my decision not to date. But, as destiny would have it, I telephoned Eric one night to speak with him and Vicki answered. She stated that Eric was away from home and left no word concerning his return. I asked her to give Eric the message that I telephoned him during his time away from home. She acquiesced and then followed by inquiring if the group would practice at her home that day.

Her voice sounded crisp and very pleasant to hear, as she proceeded to express how much she enjoyed our rehearsal the other night. I thanked her for the kudos, and then complimented her on having such a lovely voice. From there, one thing led to another, and we ended up talking on the phone for an hour. The group gathered the following evening at Eric's house and afterward, Vicki and I talked downstairs for a while, and then I left. We had several conversations inside a month's time, and things got deeper and deeper. I expressed to her my idea of being a full-fledged bachelor, since I did not have the time to give any woman. She voiced her unreadiness for marriage at that time and that made me feel even better. Now, I began to take a second look at dating her because all of the advantages seemed to have been there. First, she was a pretty girl. Secondly, I could see her after our rehearsals, and finally, I would not have to concern myself with the marriage issue. All of these things appealed to me very much, and I decided to take the ball and run with it.

After graduation, I decided to enter college, along with the influence from my mother, of course. I left St Joe's Paper Company to become a manager for Burger King. Between managing Burger King, attending college, and singing in the group, I had little or no time for my darling Vicki. I must give the *old girl* some credit for her persistent perseverance. She hung in there with me, our busy schedule with rehearsals and gigs, as well as through the bad times.

I went to college two and half years, by that time the

Atlanta Parliaments had a reputation of being the best-dressed vocal performing artists in Atlanta. We thought, it was high time for us to go in the studio and make some noise, but the capital back up did not say a mumbling word. Eventually, we joined a booking agency known as **Showcase Productions**, and a booking agent, Elliott Clark booked our engagements. He booked us out of town practically every weekend.

The Parliaments Perform at Morris Brown College

Clark matched us with an out-of-town band, *The Soul Squad*. They were nice and a clean-cut band who were dependable and strictly business. We were good for each other mainly because we were a well-disciplined group that did not get excited or respond to every mini-skirt walking by. The band *meant business* first, and everything else came later; we collaborated for about a year-and-a half, then things changed.

The Soulful Sounds of The Atlanta Parliaments

Clark started booking us with another band, called *The Soul Aces*; they were very good also, only larger in number. We had an engagement with them in South Carolina, a place called the *Playboy Club*. The people there were friendly and expressed their enthusiasm after the show ended. They repeatedly asked us when we would return, and two of the young ladies inquired if they could go with us, but of course, we gave them an emphatic, "No."

Johnny Waring, the club owner requested if we wanted another booking engagement at the club; we responded with a decisive, "Yes!" Johnny had a close friend, Joe Brown. Joe helped him every so often to run the bar, make pickups at the bus station or the airport, or even book a big-name act in town. Joe brought us from the bus station when we first arrived and now he was taking us back. He made small talk with us as we headed down the road. He asked who managed us and how long the group was currently in existence. We explained that we managed ourselves for the past seven years, and he expressed an interest in managing us. He further stated that he had an interest in us returning and becoming our financial backer. We decided to go home, think about it, and touch base with him on our next booking in that town.

We arrived in Atlanta late that night and caught a cab home. The next day, I picked Vicki up and we went to the park to relax and talk. She became very unhappy when I informed her of Joe Brown's proposition, but she was too kind and loving to stand in the way of something I wanted to do. I told her not to worry needlessly because the group had not discussed whether we would accept or reject his offer. Vicki's intuition revealed to her that not only were we going, but also we would be gone a long time. I attempted to convince her otherwise, but it seemed useless.

The following weekend, we set up a rehearsal and at the close of the practice, we decided to discuss Joe's proposition. We brainstormed on the positive and negative reasons why we should or should not go.

The Question Marks Prepare to Go On Tour

In the final analysis, all votes were unanimous for leaving town. We felt that it was time-out for singing other artists' songs. It was high time we record some of the songs that I had written. My writing had improved drastically over the months, and now it was time to put it to the test.

The Question Marks - County Hall Auditorium
Charleston SC

Chapter Nine

GROUP DEMISE

✳ ✳ ✳

It took us two weeks to make all final arrangements and say the necessary good-byes to our friends and relatives. We boarded the bus that afternoon and arrived in South Carolina that evening at ten-thirty. We called Joe Brown ahead of time, and he met us as usual. Joe was a big man that weighed anywhere from 290 to 310 pounds. He was only five feet-nine inches tall, so that made his weight stand out even more. He smoked five-dollar cigars, quite regularly, not to mention the luxurious car he drove. It was a late model, fully loaded Electra 225. To be as large as he was, Joe was a firm believer in dressing and riding in style.

He took us to a lady friend of his that had an upstairs living quarters in a decorative style. Our eyes almost popped out when we saw the place. She was a neat and clean woman with a heart of gold. I do not know how much she was charging Joe for us to stay there, but I do know one thing, it was worth every penny she charged. Joe gave us a grocery allowance to buy food every week or if he did not have cash, he would write a check. For one or two weeks, we loaded up heavy on groceries, but after that, we started saving the money that he gave us. I had a suspicion that there would be some rainy days ahead. Little did I know that a thunderstorm was on the way.

The County Hall was the auditorium used for all big name entertainers who toured through South Carolina. Joe Brown and Johnny Waring had decided to team up and promote top name acts at the County Hall and feature us as the "special added attraction". We did shows with artists such as James Brown, Tyrone Davis, Johnny Taylor, Clarence Carter, and Candi Stanton. We continued to remain well-groomed and refrained from being involved in drugs. Our wardrobe had accumulated to ten changes in uniforms with shoes to match. Things were going great. We felt as though we did not have a care in the world: only to eat, sleep, travel, and sing. What could go wrong? All points said go, and that is what we did.

The Student, Anthony and the Mentor, James Brown

The Question Marks Sing 'A Rainbow'

Our name became a household word in Charleston and we decided that it was time to do some recording in the studio. When we told Joe about our decision, he said that his money was low, but he continued to write checks. About two weeks later, he took us to the grocery store because the refrigerator was empty. Joe insisted that we load the buggy up with groceries, and he told Seal and me to take two or three items back where they belonged on the shelf.

Meanwhile, Dwight proceeded to head for the cashier with the basket of food. Joe gave him a check to pay for the items. The cashier looked at the check and asked Dwight to wait just a minute. She proceeded to phone the manager's office in the back of the store. Joe Brown eased out of sight. As he turned to go down the third aisle, Seal and I ran into him. He told us to turn around and go the other way fast. I could tell something was wrong by the look he gave and the heavy drips of sweat rolling off Joe's face.

I asked him what was wrong and all he said was, "Shut up and get out of the store fast". A sudden rage of fear filled my whole body, and my shoes felt as if they had cast iron in them. It seemed as though I could not get to the exit fast enough. When we finally reached outside to the car, Dwight still had not come out. I knew then something terrible happened. Joe slammed the door and we sped away. He drove across the street behind one of the buildings, parked, and waited silently. By this time, the spinning in my head felt like it was out of control and stars seem to appear before my very eyes. As if, this had been some dreadful nightmare.

It was no dream though. It was the *real McCoy*. Just then, two police cars pulled into the parking lot of the store with their blue lights flashing. I looked helplessly with tears in my eyes and Seal kept shaking his head. At that very moment, I thought about Eric, who decided at the last minute to go to the barbershop, instead of going with us.

The police were inside the store for only five minutes, and

when they came out, they had Dwight in handcuffs, lowering his head as he entered the paddy wagon. When they drove off, Joe waited two minutes and drove to the barbershop to get Eric. Eric's first question was, "Where is Dwight?" I told him to wait and I would tell him later.

Meanwhile, Joe told us to get out of town and not to worry about Dwight because he would get him out. Joe asked if we had enough money to get out of town, and we told him no. He reached into his coat pocket, pulled out more blank checks, and told us to write it for the amount we needed to catch a plane. Joe took off in his car, and we jumped into our *Ford Galaxie* that he purchased for us. I quickly shredded the blank checks he gave us because I perceived then he was up to no good. If any more bad checks were written, they would have to come from the source, Joe Brown. This had placed us in enough hot water already.

Although, we had enough money in our treasury, Joe Brown had no knowledge of it. We decided that we were not going to leave until we could find out what happened to Dwight. We went to a motel and rented a room for the night. We sat down, discussed the current situation, and made a decision to convey what transpired with someone that we all trusted. We considered sharing this with Joe's brother, who managed *Joe's Cab Company* for him. We soon canceled that idea.

Finally, we thought about Mr. White, a club owner who was fond of the group. Surely, he would help us. We drove to his club that night, and when we got there, I began to have a strange sixth sense that something was not right. However, I casually ignored it. Mr. White greeted us and we sat and told him of our terrible experience. He was not shocked at all, that meant he probably knew of Joe's derogatory past. He demanded that we gather our things, come, and stay with him. He owned and managed a boarding house; it was a very large spread. His hired help drove us back to the motel to collect our luggage, and check out. Then we headed back to the boarding house.

The next morning, we awoke to the fresh smell of fish, grits, and eggs coming from the kitchen. Eric was already up and gone to the bathroom. When he returned, he had a worried look on his face. He paused for a second and checked outside the door to ensure that no one was listening. He gathered the three of us and whispered, "When I went to the bathroom, I overheard Mr. White talking to a man, and the man told him to keep the group here until further instructions". No doubt that man was none other than yours truly, Joe Brown. I did not realize how much power and control Joe Brown had in this town until now. Evidently, Mr. White had his price, just like everyone else.

We decided that we could help Dwight better if we left town and sought help from people we knew, but how could we get our luggage in the car without them seeing or hearing us. It seemed virtually impossible to us, there was too much luggage, and the risk was too great. We decided to leave with the shirts on our backs and sneaked out to our car, released the brake, and eased off quietly. We arrived at the airport and took a stand-by flight to Atlanta.

Boy, Atlanta had never looked and felt so good. It was a far cry from the dreary atmosphere left behind. A cab dropped us off at Eric's house and we found out that the news was already out upon our arrival. We sat, recounted the story to his family, and then telephoned Dwight's mother. Mrs. Hunt arrived within the hour and we gave her all the details. She received it very well. She was always a sweet and understanding person. She and her husband made plans to go get Dwight. I spoke to the group about our returning to Charleston with them, but there were positively no volunteers. I decided to accompany them by myself. It was not an easy decision to make, nevertheless, I put my trust in the Lord.

We rode the bus to Charleston, which was an eight-hour ride, including layovers. I bought two hamburgers and ate one of them before boarding the bus. I took my seat as the bus pulled off, and my stomach began to bubble. I immediately knew what was happening. The fast food restaurant failed to cook the hamburger meat thoroughly or it spoiled already. I went to the restroom at the rear of the bus and threw up repeatedly, breakfast, lunch, and dinner.

I sealed off the restroom, and no one could enter. People knocked repeatedly on the door, but there was absolutely no entrance, for I was a total basket case. It is sad to say, but I spent eighty percent of the time in the bathroom during the whole trip. We had a layover, and Mrs. Hunt purchased a warm Coke and aspirin for me. I did not think it was a good idea, but I tried it anyway, and sure enough, it worked. When we arrived, I left the bus feeling brand new, after experiencing such a horrible illness.

We arrived at the station, and Mrs. Hunt spoke to the authorities about Dwight. They informed her that they did not believe Dwight or the group was guilty, but that Joe Brown set us up. The sergeant explained that they wanted to catch Joe Brown for a long time, but he always slipped through their fingers. He told us if we cooperated and helped them nail Joe, the charges would not stick. They arrested Joe on a suspicion charge and placed him on a five-thousand dollar bond. He was out in a day or so and back on the streets. He threatened Dwight and accused him of lying on him, but Joe's luck ran out. He ended up kidnapping a man and jumping bond, which made the picture look very dim for him. The last we heard, they had traced him somewhere over in Hong Kong, but they could not touch him over there.

We arrived back in Atlanta safely, and putting an end to the Joe Brown saga made things even better. I decided to slow down, get a steady job, and stay out of trouble. Dwight had to square things away with the Armed Forces. They had been trying to reach him and did not understand why he failed to return their messages. Eric and Seal remained idle and rather content with that, *at the moment*. Everything slowly returned to normal.

Vicki and I started courting again and I saw her on a regular basis. Elliott Clark telephoned us one weekend and wanted the group to put something together and go to Stockbridge, Georgia. He did not realize there was still a little bitterness among the group that needed time to heal. For the sake of dedication, we went to perform. After we came offstage, Dwight and Seal began to have a few words over something very small and insignificant, but that was all it took to bring the water to a boil. Before Eric and I knew anything, we had to pull them apart and stand between them.

I must say, it was *the straw that broke the camel's back;* in addition, it was the last time the group ever performed again. It crushed Eric more than anyone else and disappointed him deeply. It never entered his mind that we might break up. It took quite some time before he fully recovered, but praises to God, he made it all the way back.

Chapter Ten

MUHAMMAD ALI

✵ ✵ ✵

AND THE MOVIE

Dynamic Duo Freeman & Franklin

Somewhere down the line, Dwight and I started singing as a duo, and we called ourselves Freeman and Franklin. Subsequently, we tried to pave the path that the group established earlier and it seemed easier with just us two than the four of us. We hit all of the nightspots and the audiences loved us. We had pictures, newspaper clippings, business cards, and all. Elliott Clark booked us every week, in and out of town, and we went anywhere he booked us, except Charleston, South Carolina. We stayed active for a straight six months, during the week I managed a Church's Fried Chicken restaurant. I stayed with Church's for four years and decided to give it up and put more concentration into music.

Dwight and I performed together for two years and decided that it was time to leave Atlanta again, but this time we would sell all we possessed, and utilize our money to take us to Las Vegas. We made a decision to do one last show before leaving town and booked it at the *2001 Odyssey* downtown. We handled the advertising and all other promotions for the show, and contracted the *Wrecking Crew* as the band for that evening. Everything went smooth as silk, and we had a full house. This was an important night for Dwight and me, because this would mark our debut for doing separate shows instead of a duo.

Dwight's outfit was a two-piece red pants and jacket with white trim. His introduction title was *The Love Messenger.* That night I adorned myself in a royal blue jump suit trimmed in silver-like glitter. The jump suit, made with a hood attached to it, and my introduction title was *Mr. Mighty Love.* I refuse to go so far as to say who outdid who that night, but I will say one thing, and that is I was so proud to see Mom and Dad in the audience, along with a host of other relatives. I must also admit what a beautiful send-off it was indeed.

We left Atlanta on April 29, 1977, which was my birthday. Dwight drove his car and I drove mine, and we traveled the expressway northwest bound on I-75. We drove for three hours and stopped to refuel and rest. By nightfall, we pulled into Memphis Tennessee, and decided to call it quits for the night. We drove around sightseeing the Elvis Presley Mansion, Al Green's Church, the Memphis Stadium, et cetera. It was about eleven-thirty, and we drove past a nightclub that was jammed packed. We turned around, parked, and went inside.

The club owner greeted us, and strangely enough, his face seemed strikingly familiar. He introduced himself as Charles Allen, and treated us as his special guests for the evening. We had a long and lengthy conversation with him, and discovered not only did we have things in common, but he also was from Atlanta. That night, he invited us to his house to meet his family, and we stayed until he locked up the club, which was at five o'clock in the morning. We talked until Charles fell asleep on the couch, but by that time, our heads were on one accord, about our plans together.

Charles showed us some paperwork indicating he was a rather lucrative promoter and booking agent. He had contracted *The O'Jay's, Al Green, Freida Payne, Luther Ingram,* and many more. After five years of booking, he and his business associates divided the money, split up, and that is when he went into the nightclub business. Charles said he missed promoting and booking shows, but he needed some help and some young ideas. We teamed up and he promoted us here and there. Not only did the ladies like our act, but the men did too. Charles became so involved in promoting and traveling with us that he hired extra help to run the club in his absence.

Dwight's Brother, Michael Comes on Board

We spent two months in Memphis and began to get bored and restless, because this had not been our original plan. It was time to either move on or change our course of action. Ironically, Charles felt our vibration because he surprised us with a booking at the Rick's Armory in Little Rock, Arkansas. I had a long awaited desire to visit this city. A handful of black students made history in 1957. They made a successful attempt in integrating Central High School. I admired those students for having the courage to take a stand for their rights and the rights of others.

Rick's Armory was a round dome-shaped building that seated several thousand people and a clear view of the stage. Charles arranged for two available concession stands, in case anyone in the crowd got the munchies during the show. The band was dynamite. They called themselves, *Mack Attack*, and if you saw them perform, you would understand how they got their name. They created an excitement in the air, as they, without warning, went from one song to another.

When they announced show time, Dwight came out and sang four selections, and I followed him with five. The receptive crowd did not want us to leave and I believe some of them could stay all night, if given half a chance.

Later, when the show ended, we received numerous compliments and invitations to return. I met a photographer, a business owner; he expressed an interest in taking some pictures for my portfolio. I met another business owner of a clothing store; he expressed an interest in dressing me for future stage appearances. Last, but not the least, there was an engineer of a local studio that invited me to lay some musical tracks with him, if I was in town again.

Mr Mighty Love Sings "A Statue of A Fool"

Several business owners suggested unbelievable offers to me that night. I refused to allow myself to let them go unnoticed. Dwight and I discussed it at length, when we returned to Memphis. We shared our decision to head back to Little Rock with Charles, and to our amazement, he was a bit surprised. Without nudging, we persuaded him of our plan to remain in touch with him. He seemed visibly relieved after I conveyed that to him. We pulled out the following weekend, and Charles showed his thanks and gratitude by giving each of us a full tank of gas.

The disc jockey on the radio announced there would be free food and watermelon in the park on Saturday. I turned my radio off and asked Dwight if he had heard the announcement, and he nodded. We made plans to sleep in our cars, rise, and shine early enough for the breakfast.

The next morning, I awoke and discovered I had overslept and Dwight had left me. Tired and full of exhaustion, I did not hear his car drive off. I laid back and fell fast asleep again, waking an hour and a half later. It was eleven o'clock and the intense sunrays seemed to beam down on my car only, which was a black Chevy; I quickly moved behind the steering wheel and drove downtown to the bus station. I went into the men's rest room, washed off, and changed into some fresh clothes from the trunk of my car. I arrived at the park in time to see the sanitation workers clean up the litter and other miscellaneous items.

Boy was I hungry and thirsty. It hit me all of a sudden that I had not eaten in almost twenty hours. The more I thought about it, the hungrier I became. My vision became an instant radar for anything that looked or smelled like food, but all I lucked up on was a water fountain. Man, I never knew water could taste so good. As I drank continuously, someone began tapping me on my shoulder.

I rose up, gasped for breath, and heard someone say, "Good gracious, man, are you going to drink the fountain dry?" I turned around, it was Dwight, and he was dressed in a blue three-piece suit. I expressed how hungry I was, and he said he was full of watermelon. He said he did not want to wake me this morning because I was sleeping so soundly.

I said, "Ha, a likely story". Dwight filled me in on some of the people he had met at the park, and everything he said went in one ear and out the other, until he mentioned that someone invited us to dinner. He met the manager of the *Razorback Movie Theater* and told him that we were in the *Muhammad Ali* movie. Somehow, the manager thought Dwight was referring to another picture, titled *Muhammad, Messenger of God.*

As Dwight was talking, I began to reminisce over the wonderful opportunity we experienced, one that I would never forget. It had been almost five months since the group had broken up, and Dwight and I would from time to time check out some of the hotspots in Atlanta. Only this time, I decided to go to the "Silver Fox Club" alone. It had been only two hours, when a man came out and made an announcement seeking talented individuals to take part in a movie. The movie was entitled, *The Greatest,* and there was a party scene scheduled for a shoot downtown at the Hyatt *Regency* Hotel next week. He urged everyone who had an interest to go downtown in the morning and sign up for a part.

Well, I guess a lot of the people that night thought this

guy was crazy or had had one or two too many drinks. I could tell immediately that he was on the level, and without a moment to lose, I called Dwight. He was asleep, of course, but he became wide-awake when I shared with him the news.

It was three o'clock in the morning, and I acted as though it was high noon, but success is that way sometimes. You got to answer when it knocks on your door. I picked him up at four in the morning, and we rode down to the hotel to get an early start. Sure enough, *Muhammad Ali's* training team was in the breakfast area downstairs eating with the casting director and camera crew. We introduced ourselves, sat down, and drank a cup of coffee with them.   The director seemed very nice, he reminded me of *Yul Brynner*. His hairstyle was similar, if you know what I mean. He immediately took to my personality for some reason, and he asked me if he could call me Tony. Of course, I said yes. We discussed the movie scene and his life style. Suddenly, he popped the question.

"Hey, how would you guys like to have a speaking part in this movie?"

"Are you kidding? We would love it."

"Well, I'll see what I can do about that. Oh, and by the way, would you fellows happen to know anyone with some 1970 automobiles? If so, bring them by and let us consider whether we can use them in the movie. We had planned to allow a week before shooting, but the response has been so tremendous that we decided to start shooting day after tomorrow."

"Hey, that's right on-time. I think we can come up with a white-on-white *Coupe de Ville* by then."

"Well, what are you guys waiting for? High-tail it out there and rustle me up some cars."

Dwight and I walked back to my car and sat for a moment in disbelief at what just occurred. We thought this might be our big chance to make it big. The director told us that our pay was one hundred dollars for our speaking parts and a hundred fifty for each car used in the movie. The only person I could think of right then, who had a 1970 car was my old friend Tony Ross. I wasted no time going to his home to pay him a quick visit. I saw Tony watering the lawn as I drove up to the curb in front of his house; we greeted each other, made small talk, and finally talked over the reason I dropped by to see him.

I asked him if I could trade my *'73 Caprice* for his *'70* Coupe de Ville for two days, and without batting an eye, he said, "Why sure, man. What's mine is yours and what's yours is mine." Tony probably speculated that I wanted to use it to impress some cute chick, so I made him none the wiser about it. Tony's "ride," back then was known as a white-on-white in white hog. It was a soft top with leather interior, and I must add, it was well preserved for a six-year-old model. I let down the top and drove off.

After Dwight finished casing the interior, he said, "Freeman, what about your friend, Bear Smith?"

"Who?"

"You know, Max 'Bear' Smith, the boxer, the guy who delivered your chickens to *Church's Chicken.*"

"Oh yeah, I had forgotten all about him."

I had told Max if I ever had a chance to talk to *Muhammad Ali*, I would try to set up a try-out for Ali's training camp.

Dwight and I had always been close fans of the champ and we watched his career flourish from the time he was a youngster to when he was a young man. I felt he would give Max a break, if I could get to him and talk with him. We drove back to the hotel to let the director see the car, and he approved it on the spot. He told us to have the car back the next day at 9:00 p.m. for the shooting.

We asked Bundini Brown, who at the time was Ali's coach, if he thought Ali would spar a few rounds with a local fighter here in town. He said, "Sure, go get him; we'd like to see him".

We left immediately for Max's house. When we arrived, his wife told us he was at the gym working out. We left and went to the **Ollie Street Gym**, and we found him sparring.

"When he sat down to rest, I went over to talk to him.

"How's everything going, Max?"

"Freeman! Dude, it has been a long time. Are you doing okay?"

"Yeah, Max, I've been doing pretty well. Look here, Max, I'd like for you to meet my singing partner, Dwight Franklin."

"Hey, Dwight, what's happening, man?"

"Glad to meet you, Max. Freeman has told me a lot about you."

"Uh, man, it's nothing. I am just trying to make a living. Ain't that right, Mike? Look here, Mike, this is Freeman, the cat I told you about who managed the chicken store, out on **Old National Highway**."

"Hey Freeman, I've heard a lot about you too, man. Max told me that you could blow something terrible."

"Well Mike, what can I say other than it's a living. Max, I

guess you're wondering what brings me on this side of town. Well, do you remember, about two years ago, I told you if ever I got a chance to talk to Muhammad Ali, I would be sure and tell him about you? Well, Ali is in town shooting his movie *The Greatest*, and his coach said he would probably consider giving you a try-out, that is, if you look good enough. He asked us to bring you down so he can take-a-look at you. So, Max, what do you say? Max!"

"Uhhhuh, huh? Max stammered, "What did you say?"

"Do you want this chance or not, man?"

"Freeman, I'm sorry for daydreaming, but I just can't believe that this really happening to me. I've waited so long to make it until I thought it just wasn't meant to be."

Well, it will never happen if we don't hurry up and get back to *Regency*."

"The *Regency*!"

"Yeah, that's where the movie is being shot."

"Well, what are we waiting for? Let's go."

Bundini paced the floor when we got back. He probably got bored with things, seeing how there had been no real action in the ring for quite some time. He took one look at Max, as if, sizing him up for the kill, and said, "He'll do just fine, if he can take a punch. Felipe, how long will it be before Ali comes down?"

I don't know, Bundini. The last I heard his hands were hurting him."

"Well, send someone up to tell him that there's a young lad here who wants to spar a few rounds with him."

Boy, did we get excited as curiosity filled the air. People were asking who this Max "Bear" Smith was. Fifteen minutes-later, a man came down and said that Ali agreed to box three rounds with Max tomorrow morning at eleven-thirty. Bundini asked if there was a place nearby where this bout could take place and Max immediately told him that he could take care of the arrangements. We left casually and when we got to the car, we exploded in an uproar of happiness. We could not wait for tomorrow, for it was sure to change the lives of all of us. I told Max to let it be known to any interested party that he was under a verbal contract with *Freeman and Franklin*. I also gave him orders to go home, take a nice hot bath, and relax until tomorrow. He told me that's what he was going to do.

The next morning at nine-thirty, I called Max, and he gave me a bit of bad news. He told me he had gone out to the gym after all, and overworked himself and now his legs were sore and tight as drums. My first impulse was to react with harsh anger, but I thought for ten seconds and calmed down. I told Max I would be right over. I went to the store, picked up some *Ben Gay*, and drove to Max's house. His wife was pacing the floor when I came to the door.

She said, "Hello, Anthony, he's in here." She pointed to the back bedroom. When I entered the room, Max was lying flat on his back, barely able to move.

I bent down to feel the tightness of his legs and he cried," Freeman, I'm sorry. I know I let you down, but I couldn't help it. I got more and more nervous last night and somewhere along the line I panicked and started working out like crazy. I didn't realize the damage I had done until this morning."

I tried to talk with compassion and a little confidence as I said, "Hey, Max, it's all right. I probably would have done the same thing, but I hope not all is lost. You just lie still and let me work on you a bit." I wasted no time going to work on Max. I massaged and beat his legs and life slowly began to come back in them. I helped Max until he could stand, and I continued to massage and beat his legs as he walked. It was soon eleven o'clock, and amazingly Max had gained confidence. Victory had not been lost yet, at least not without a fight.

We stopped to get Dwight on our way, and nothing was said of what had transpired. We arrived at the *Regency* at exactly eleven-thirty and when we went inside, Ali's training team was waiting in the lobby. Everyone was there, except *Muhammad Ali*. Bundini Brown came up to us and asked if we were ready. We told him yes. He said that Muhammad Ali's hands were giving him problems and instead, a former champion named *Jimmy Ellis* would take his place, that is, if it were all right with us. Bundini assured us everything would still be on the up and up, because they merely wanted to see if Max could take a punch and Jimmy's word would be valid to Ali. We agreed and everybody carpooled to the *Butler Street YMCA*.

We pulled up to the gym and only a few people were there, but the word went out like wildfire that *Jimmy Ellis* was about to fight and over two hundred people were there in a flash. The director of the gym was excited and most cooperative and he even went so far as to put up a make-believe ring for us. Ellis's entire training team was in his corner, and Dwight and I were in Max's corner.

The fight opened up with Jimmy throwing a left and a right to Max's head. Max covered up, and Jimmy immediately began to dominate the fight. Jimmy slipped several punches to the inside of Max's stomach, causing his legs to buckle, but the bell rang *in the nick of time.* The fighters went to their corners and took a two-minute rest.

In the course of those two minutes, I began talking to Max very seriously, and I told him he had to do all he could to take this next round, because I figured Jimmy definitely was not going to let him have the first or the last round. The bell sounded for the second round, and Max surprised us all by running over to Jimmy's corner, connecting immediately. He kept Jimmy off balance for a minute and a half. Jimmy got back in the swing of things, but it was too late, for Max had stolen the round. The bell sounded to end the round, and Jimmy looked angry as he eyed his opponent in his corner.

Max came to his corner soaked in sweat and exhausted. He told me that his legs had started to cramp on him. I started beating and massaging them, but there just was not enough time. The bell sounded for the third and final round, so I instructed him to maintain his position for the remainder of the round. Jimmy came in with all he had, bobbing and weaving, counter-punching, and looking for any sign of weakness. He kept Max off-balance the entire round, but did not knock him out. The bell sounded, ending the third round, and our corner jumped with joy, for our mission was finally accomplished. We proved that we could take a punch.

Max went in the locker room to change, and Dwight and I stayed in the gym waiting for him, figuring up the money we would make in the future. After twenty minutes had gone by, and Max had not come out, we became suspicious. We went to the locker room, and it was empty. When we got outside, all the cars were gone. By that time, we had put two and two together, jumped in our car, and drove to the hotel. Upon our arrival to the *Regency*, we were unable to find a single soul. We hopped on the elevator and canvased every floor; however, there was no one in sight anywhere. We sat waiting for an hour. Finally, everybody appeared from a room upstairs, everyone except Max that is. We asked Bundini where Max was, and he told us the room number.

When we got there, Max was talking to Don King's right-hand man, C. B. Atkins, and though we had not seen him in all this time, I could tell he was one of the biggies who handled the big-money deals. We sat down, talked for a few minutes, and discovered our boxer had signed a contract *with Don King Productions*. We were upset and told the agent that we contracted Max and that all the negotiations were required to go through us. He asked Max if he was cognizant of the verbal agreement when he signed, and Max said yes, but he did not think it would interfere with the matter.

The agent said, although our verbal contract would not hold up in court, he was willing to give us finder's fee rights. We made negotiations to receive a hundred thousand dollars after Max's fourth fight. We had to settle for that or nothing at all. Max had a contract and that was what really counted. They told Max to sit tight and they would send for him in two weeks.

That night we did the party scene, and everything was fabulous at the *Regency*. The director had the crowd chant, *"Ali, Ali, Ali"*, and the champ made his way down the glass elevator. After the scene took place, the director called for the skit that they prepared for Dwight, Felipe, and me. At first, I thought the director had forgotten about the speaking parts, but things turned out just the opposite. It took us four times to run through the skit before it was a print.

The next day, the crew went out to Senator Leroy Johnson's house to shoot some more footage, and three days after that they were gone. Max waited patiently for two weeks, three weeks, and during that time, *Don King Productions* had been accused of rigging some of their bouts. The press and the boxing commission had them under heavy scrutiny. The timing for all of this to happen could not have been worse, for it knocked Max right out of the driver's seat.

There was a clause in the contract giving them the option of cancellation through a non-contract and that is exactly what Max received. Although Max's pride was hurt, along with ours, he still managed to pull himself together and went back to delivering chickens. Dwight and I dusted ourselves off, and started working on our next project. Even though, we had lost a boxer, we looked forward to the upcoming premier of the movie. It was scheduled to come out in three months, but before two months passed, the director died, and our dream went up in smoke. Whoever replaced him as director edited us right out of the film.

"Freeman, Freeemmaann."

"Uh, yeah?"

"Partner, I don't know where your mind was, but I can tell it was far away."

"Oh, I'm sorry, Dwight. I was going through a bit of nostalgia. Now what was that you were saying?"

"Forget it, man. Let's go eat."

Chapter Eleven

THE FUND-RAISING

Dwight led the way to the manager's house, and when we arrived, everything was laid out very nicely. This guy really thought we were superstars, because he had his best china and silverware out. He was a respectable person and went out of his way to insure we were comfortable. He introduced us to his wife, whose name was Melody. She was attractive, but the prime ribs she placed on the table looked even better. Her menu consisted of four different types of vegetables, and the bread was homemade.

After we had finished the delicious meal, it dawned on me that Dwight failed to introduce us. To keep from being embarrassed, I said, "Excuse me, if you don't mind would it be all right to drop the formalities, and just call each other by our first names?"

"Why sure, I'd love that even better. Just call me Jack."

"All right, Jack, you can feel free to call me Anthony, and I think you already know Dwight's first name. Don't *'cha?*"

"Yes, I know old Dwight. Okay, now that we have

everything out of the way, I guess we'd better get down to the radio station and advertise your visit to Little Rock."

Jack took us to the radio station. We went on the air, told the listeners that we were in town, and would sign autographs at the theater. When the theater opened, we were standing at the entrance as the people walked in, and we both were dressed to kill. After about two hours, two beautiful young ladies appeared at the entrance, causing all heads to turn. I figured they were sisters since their lovely complexion were so closely matched. They paid the clerk, and as they approached us, I selected the lady of my choice and greeted her by kissing the back of her hand. Stunned, she immediately began blushing. I took advantage of the situation and introduced myself, giving her an autographed picture. I asked her name, since she did not volunteer the information.

She introduced herself as Doris and said the other one's name was Mary. Dwight and I both knew we would stand at the entrance for the rest of the week and nothing would come close to matching these two pearls. We kindly escorted the ladies to their seats and joined them; we chatted with them for a few minutes, until movie time. Mary asked Dwight to point out our acting roles in the movie. I suddenly excused myself to the men's room.

Dwight came about five minutes later and said, "Freeman, we've got to figure out something and fast, because those ladies are pretty smart, especially Mary. She told me she figured this whole thing was a hoax from the very beginning."

"What did you say?"

"Well, I told her to be patient and our parts were near the end."

"Good thinking, Dwight. Now all we have to do is to figure out what parts in the movie to pick out that would pass for you and me. I'll tell you what Dwight, if there is a fight scene in the movie, we can say we are two of the extras in the background."

"Yeah man, that's a good idea. Let's hurry and get back to our seats before they think we chickened out."

As Dwight said, Mary was definitely a smart person. When the fight scene came we pointed ourselves out in the background, which was almost impossible to see, and she called us both liars. She told Dwight if he did not confess, she was going to report it to the manager. Dwight appeared alarmed at the threat Mary made, he confessed, and then apologized. Mary burst out with laughter at the fear she put in both of us. Although it was not funny at the time, we deserved every bit of it.

The movie ended, we asked for their addresses and phone numbers and said good-bye. Dwight and I talked about what a nice time we had with them and how they struck us as being different from other women we had met. We did not visit them immediately. We thought it was best not to visit them for a while.

Each morning, we drove to the bus station to refresh ourselves. This soon became a regular routine for us, and it became obvious by the desk clerk's expression that he did not approve. One particular morning, as we prepared to leave the bus station, Dwight met a guy named Michael. Mike empathized with our situation and invited us to stay at his parents' home for a few days. He said they were out of town, but would return shortly.

We moved in long enough to establish a forwarding address and immediately had our lady friends back home send us money. Rev. Caldwell and his wife arrived home and Mike was out at the time, so we had to explain to them who we were and why we were there. I must say that they were most hospitable under the circumstances and we will never forget them.

Vicki baked two and a half pounds of some delicious cookies and mailed them to our current address, along with some money, of course. As I look back at that year of uncertainty, it reminds me how grateful and thankful we were to receive those gifts. At the end of all Vicki's letters, she would write, *P.S. Send for me.* Maybe one day I would send for her, but I *knew,* that it would not be any time soon. We resided with the Caldwells for approximately two weeks; Dwight and I knew the time had come to leave, but we stopped by from time to time, and picked up whatever mail we had received.

We went back to the street, which was a drag, but we did not have a choice. We slept in our cars, as usual, but we changed locations. Each morning, the sun would beat down upon our cars leaving us no choice, but to get up and get out. After a while, our gas tanks began to get low, but we refused to request any more money from back home. We decided to use the two containers that the cookies arrived in and solicit funds from people in shopping malls and grocery parking areas. Boy was it hot and humid, not to mention the long hours we endured. Somehow, we managed to persevere, until we had acquired enough money to sustain us for a while.

One day while in the grocery store shopping, we stumbled

across Mary and Doris, the two sisters we had met at the theater. They were *tickled pink* to see us, and we were happy too. They invited us to their home and prepared a nice home cooked meal for us. We ate and then went into the den to watch television. Mary and Doris were two gregarious individuals, who were reared very well by two loving parents whom anyone would cherish. They had a foundational Christian background, which they had yet to stray. They opened up their homes to us, as if we were members of their family. Yes, I learned from these two ladies the true meaning of being a Christian. It is the sacrificial giving of oneself unconditionally to others and without expecting something in return, feeding, clothing, sharing, and caring for God's children.

Chapter Twelve

DAMASCUS ROAD

It was now August, Dwight and I were both working, earning an honest wage. I felt good. We rented an apartment together for a while, and then Dwight moved three doors down from me. Now, that things were back in the proper perspective, we were again able to perform in nightclubs. Mary and Doris joined us one evening at an engagement and were astounded to find out we could perform. They soon realized we were not just talk. In a very short time, we had sifted through some of the best musicians in Little Rock and formed a remake of the old group called "Superstars". I began writing songs again during lunch hour while on the job. God was blessing me and there was improvement in my writing skills and talent. I managed to write over seventy-five songs with succinct progress during that time.

I finally contacted those business people whom I had met at *Rick's Armory*, and they all were interested in doing something with my talent. My lawyer Manuel Pruitt, the photographer John Miller, the clothing-store dealer McWalker, and the studio engineer Jerry Wilson got together to form a corporation based on how to make Anthony Freeman a successful entertainer. Prior to this, Jerry Wilson had just finished engineering a production of three songs of mine, but they were still in demo-tape form. He and I were very pleased with the outcome of the demos, so we let the other investors listen to the tape. Their reactions proved that they were sold on the product. Now, the question no longer was did I have something to sell, but rather, how to get my foot in the door.

John Miller said that he had a colleague in New York who had an affirmative-action advertising business and it was only *a drop in the hat* to print some brochures, T-shirts, flyers, et cetera. Everyone seemed full of ideas about how to get me through the door, but saying it and doing it were two different things. At this point, I was *on a roll* and felt that nothing could stop me. These guys were businessmen, and certainly, they would prevent anything from hindering my success. We scheduled two other meetings, and things were on a positive note, that is, up until the following meeting.

Everyone was present except my leading investor and he did not call or leave word with anyone. We became concerned when he failed to show up for work at his photo shop. It was three long days before anyone located him, and then we found out the dreadful news. He and his wife were divorcing, and she was taking him to the laundry and the cleaners. She was asking for the house, the Mercedes, and over one hundred-fifty thousand dollars in currency. The news hit me and everyone else like a ton of bricks, for we all were dependent on John's lion share of the investment. Progress, at that point, took on a bleak appearance, which led me to believe the conquest at hand would be remote, to say the least.

After the unfortunate incident, MacWalker decided to pull out and invest his money in another clothing store on Main Street. That left my lawyer and me, and I had a determination that refused to let me give up my dream.

I began working two jobs, one as a bellman and another one pressing pants for *Levi Strauss*. I did as much overtime as possible to raise the money I needed to launch my career. When I earned what I considered a nice sum, I contacted Jerry Wilson. We sat down and figured up the cost of doing nine songs.

Luckily, it was within my budget, and we were able to start immediately. I hired musicians, female and male vocalist, extra instrument sounds that we needed, and I arranged to coordinate them for recording. It was roughly three weeks before we were ready for the mix and we finished in two days. After we completed everything, I stood back in awe at what I had accomplished. I had arranged, produced, written, published, and designed the label for the first 45 release. I also had contracts in Nashville that pressed the records, printed my business cards, and duplicated my pictures.

Things were going well, and I wanted someone to share my joys with me, so I sent for Vicki. She could not believe her ears when I told her. The dream she had waited for so long was now about to become a reality. She was due to arrive in five days, but the strangest thing happened. For some strange reason, I began to have an anxiety attack over her arrival. For two straight nights at my job, my stomach churned like butter or felt like butterflies, which kept me in an emotional state.

Little Rock Bound: Anthony Makes Vicki's Dream Come True
Lila, Anthony& Vicki

Later that night, my emotions seemed mixed with an apprehensive feeling, and I asked my supervisor if he would give me three days off, to take care of an emergency. He agreed that I did not look good and told me to take the rest of the week off work.

I left for Atlanta that night and arrived early that morning. Vicki was at work and had no idea that I was in town. When I tracked her down, she was shocked and completely bewildered at the sudden appearance of mine. To be honest, I was surprise at my actions also. I could not explain this aggressive forwardness, which unraveled in my being. We walked together to the lounge area of the bank's operations center and I hugged and kissed her. I asked her to get off work early and pack what she could of her belongings, because we had to leave that night.

By this time, her head was really spinning because things were moving too fast. The furniture that needed moving was not. She needed to pack her clothes, the mail forwarded and transferred permanently, the going-away party canceled, and the good-byes skipped, except her immediate family. There were so many things floating around in her mind that had been or that needed to be, and now would never get done. Many of her things left behind. We left at midnight and arrived in Little Rock the next morning. Vicki realized the difficulty she would have in making an adjustment in the small city. But, if it meant being together, then she felt it was worth it all.

Making Adjustments Together at Last

I continued steadfastly in my music, and Vicki was there to support me in whatever I wanted do. I knew she did not always approve, but she would quietly go along with the program. She always asked me to study the word of God with her, but I could never find the time, so she would continue to study by herself. My spiritual mind wanted to study, but my carnal mind said, *To hell with it all.* I am going to be an international recording artist.

Drivin Me Crazy Anthony's First 45 Release Record

My records soon arrived from Nashville, along with my pictures, brochures, flyers, et cetera. I was now ready to promote and sell the people on my product. I first went to the radio stations and asked them to play the record. I managed to get only one station in Little Rock to play the song and they would only play it on weekends. I tried to pay them to play the record, but in their book, that was no dice.

I went to Atlanta and gave all of my DJ friends several copies, and they promised to play it, but that was as far as their promises went. I stopped in Memphis and dropped off two thousand copies with my dear friend Charles Allen. He, in turn, took some of the records to Mississippi and distributed them among the DJ's there. After two months elapsed and nothing was happening, I got desperate and took to the streets. I went to all of the discos and had them play the record, but still nothing would click for me.

I was about to give up, when one evening I received a

long distance call from Chicago. It was a man named Hank Williams and he said that my song was listed in *Jack the Rapper* newspaper as being number one. This paper was a primary circulation amongst the radio and disco jocks. He told me if I were not under contract with anyone, he would like me to fly up there and perhaps discuss a future with his company. He told me about a DJ named Lasey Jones, who liked my music and would be willing to work with us out of Little Rock.

By this time, stars were in my eyes and everything he said sounded and seemed like the real *McCoy*. I told Vicki, when I made it, we would get married. I thought the time was ripe for me to keep that promise. Because, at this point, no one in his or her right mind could tell me that I was not about to make it big time. That night I rounded up a preacher and one or two witnesses, and we were married.

Needless to say, I went to Chicago and entered into a contract with *Soundtrack Records,* but after six months, nothing had materialized. The company I was with merged with another company and all of their material was put on hold. It had been nine months since I had signed with them, and I was fed up with the whole thing. If it meant the forfeiture of the master tape, I wanted out and that was it.

That day I made a solemn vow to yield my life to Jesus, to witness to others, and to put Christ first in all I do. This was easily said, but when I tried to put it into action, that is when I ran into the problems. First, finding a church that I felt at home was not as easy as I thought and secondly the problems involved in turning the nightlife a loose. Satan shot his arrows left and right, but I refused to give up.

One Sunday morning, Vicki and I were so depressed from the weight of the bills and other difficulties that began to transpire, that I did not know what to do. I told her that we were going to church, and at that time, I had no idea what church we would attend. We had visited many, but none had touched our hearts or made us feel a part of the body. We just jumped in the car, started driving, and the Lord led us to St. John Missionary Baptist Church. How do I know that He led us there? Well, when Pastor C. Dennis Edwards stated that the title of the sermon was **Depression**, I knew then that it could not have been anyone else, but the Lord.

From that day forward, the Lord began to change and direct my life. It was not an overnight process, but God Almighty had planted the seed. Then, through prayer, patience, and trust in the Lord, there was no longer a lustful desire to be an international star. Jesus empowered and gave me the ability to take self and put it on the shelf, and to let him as my Lord govern my life. The years of denial that I lived through, refusing to accept the fact that I was handicapped, changed also. Jesus revealed to me that I needed to reject and overcome the shame I felt, and rejoice and give thanks for the miracle *He* allowed to take place in my life. Above all, I needed to share the miracle with others. For in the book of James it reads, *"But wilt thou know, O vain man, that faith without works is dead:" (James 2:20).* The truth of the matter is that the faith that I had operated in my past and reflected in my life appeared outwardly one way, but inwardly full of dead men's bones. This observation made it paramount for me to learn to read and meditate on the word of God for myself and acknowledge those faith principles therein. Sure enough, after putting these principles into practice, my faith walk became fruitful day by day, enabling me to take a positive stand against the different pressures that were becoming increasingly apparent in the free enterprise market.

A job that I applied for over a month ago finally came through for me, at a company named *Orbit Valve*. It was a twenty-year-old business, which had established itself as a multimillion-dollar industry. Its primary focus was the manufacturing of valves for oil wells. I started out earning a decent paycheck, not to mention the outstanding benefits. *Orbit* could easily afford to keep their employees on a lucrative paying scale. During this particular time, there was an oil embargo causing the price of oil to increase to an alarming seventy-five dollars per barrel. This enabled *Orbit* to retail their valves at three or four times worth its value. Many service stations, mainly proprietors had to fold and seek other employment, while only the large corporations had the ability to sustain themselves under the iron foot of the embargo. During this era, *OPEC* was in a position to reap hefty windfall profits and was determined not to usurp price increases at the pumps. The embargo soon began to affect big businesses across the board. Companies responded by laying-off employees by the hundreds. Before America could bat an eye, she found herself bombarded with double-digit inflation, high unemployment, and exasperating interest rates. Companies all around us had to streamline their work force; while on the other hand, *Orbit* enjoyed large pay increases, rapid job advancement, bonus checks, and increases in hiring. For four years straight, *Orbit* strutted like a peacock, accepting little or no warnings of the signs of the time.

I accepted every promotion that was offered me and merely rode with the escalating wave. The wave eventually leveled off at the thirty-three level, which was top pay. This level opened up a new world for me, because I had never trained in this area before. Nevertheless, they gave me plenty of time and I had a willingness to learn. My assignment was in the dual machine department and I worked in that area for four years. Even though, there were stressful moments, I enjoyed my work. By this time, *Orbit* did so well that even most of the employees developed a mentality that the company was invincible against the system.

Orbit implemented a program that the Japanese practiced for a long time called *Quality Circles*. This was a volunteer program, by which, employees identified, analyzed, and brainstormed to find solutions to problems in their work area. Management then reviewed the problems and their research documentations. This in turn afforded them the right to accept or repudiate the solutions submitted. However, they very seldom refused to accept any documented findings due to the competent leadership that reigned over the program. This leadership comprised of two facilitators, Virginia Lowe and Debbie Oxford. They were two employees who elected to step out on faith in an area of substance. Through their belief and creativity, they were able to achieve successful results. Through their efforts, they established a liaison between management and shop workers, and they were instrumental in opening the lines of communications amongst the employees.

Three years and six months later, suddenly the unexpected occurred. Oil prices began dropping drastically, causing frustration, and fear to plague those that reaped the windfall profits ever since the embargo was enacted. The report stated that other foreign countries had successfully drilled for oil, one being Saudi Arabia, and were selling it on the open market at a reduced price. This caused *OPEC* to reap that which they had sown, which led to a more stabilized economy.

Orbit Valve was one of the companies that was on the receiving end of this shock treatment. It stripped them of their invulnerability and brought them and their employees to a place of mortification. *Orbit* suffered layoff after layoff, which ultimately resulted in making their night shift extinct.

However, even before this total collapse of the night shift, I had detected a sense of anger, bitterness, and sometimes hate disguised in the subliminal atmosphere. This detection manifested itself just prior to the second layoff, when rumors and innuendos ran rampant. In light of this episode, I became additionally perceptive to the benefits of *Quality Circles*. For as its membership began to grow, I could not help but notice that the people were joining for reasons other than solving area problems, but rather work relations with supervisors and lead men. Discussions at some of the circle meetings were most informative, significant, and profitable. However, good things have a tendency to always end, and that is precisely what happened. *Orbit* discontinued the *Quality Circles* program abruptly without warning, tagging it with an indiscreet explanation.

Now, seven years had passed since my employment with *Orbit Valve*, and never had I experienced such a depressive environment as that which was fostered. It had become much more than a chore to enter the workplace on a daily basis. Many employees, some with ten or twelve years of service, signed up for the volunteer layoff, and I was one of those employees. In addition, as fate would have it, I did not leave with that layoff group, and *oh how disappointed I was.* Nevertheless, I remained confident that my turn would come eventually.

Chapter Thirteen

A MOTHER'S LOVE

In the year 1985, the Lord continued to bring blessings my way, and life was changing more and more toward the Christian walk. It was in Little Rock where my Damascus Road experience occurred, and I will never forget that as long as I live. Just as God delivered the Israelites from Egyptian slavery, he also delivered me from the bondage of sin that Satan had over me.

Satan then began attacking my family with disease and illness. My mother had been a victim of breast cancer over twenty years ago and suffered the loss of a breast. Now twenty years later, the cancer reappeared. Only this time, it was in full bloom and waging war on her lungs. My grandmother attempted to play nursemaid to my mother. In the process, she was stricken with a stroke. It left her with a pacemaker and underweight.

The circulation of the illnesses went from my family to Vicki's family, back and forth. Between April and December of 1985, we made five to six emergency visits to Atlanta from

Arkansas, due to deaths or illnesses. Vicki and I were in the process of gathering plans for our dream house when suddenly these illnesses emerged. I immediately called my mother and asked if she thought I should move back to Atlanta, and help take care of her. Of course, she said no, with a sound of confidence and pride, which alerted me to the fact that I had a family to rear and my own life to live.

I paused for a few seconds, thinking of how much I loved her and wanted to be there for her. Then I told her in a calm, but serious voice, if she needed me, all she had to do was to call me, and I would drop everything and come running.

It was a week later, and I was in our room lying down when the phone rang. It was my mother, and boy was I surprised, for normally we communicated every two weeks. I sensed she had something important to tell me, and I was right. She asked me if I would come home and without hesitation, I told her yes. My eyes welled with tears because I knew that her failing health condition was terminal. I told her when she could expect the move to take place, which was February of the following year. She asked me to come and spend Christmas with her. I shared it with Vicki and the boys, and we decided that it was best if I went alone. After all, it had only been three weeks since we traveled to Atlanta for Thanksgiving. Satan was doing his best to accumulate negative thoughts in my mind as to why I should not go back. However, in spite of the negative influence, the Holy Spirit overpowered him, and gave me a burning desire to persevere.

I arrived a week before Christmas, and I called Jap, who had now served eighteen years in the Air Force. I told him what Mother requested and he decided to meet me there. It was truly a joy to see the whole family together for Christmas, since all of us had not been together in over ten years. Freida, whom I could no longer call my little sister, was now nineteen and a sophomore at Georgia State. I thank God my mother decided to have another child late in life, because it gets lonely when your kids grow up and leave home. I retained the title of being the Baby of the family for fourteen years, then came Freida. I gladly passed the title on to her. As the first and only girl in our immediate family, Freida received the best of everything. One might say she was spoiled rotten.

Freida and my mother had some great times together in her earlier years. They did things together and spent time with one another, while daddy drove a cab. All went well up until Freida decided it was time for her to start dating boys. A dispute occurred that created a wedge between the two of them. Freida retreated to her room for days sometimes without speaking, and feelings were never resolved among them. As a result, things only became worse. There were times when I felt sorry for Freida, because after all, she was now nineteen years old and in full bloom. Still, that made no difference to Mother, because at the time, some lunatic went around killing young and innocent black boys. It was rumored that a guy named Wayne Williams was the police's number one suspect, and had been arrested for questioning. Williams made headlines for days, and eventually he was convicted for two of the murders.

After Christmas, Jap and I made sure Mother was comfortable and well-nourished before we left. She began to show signs of recovery from that day forward, which made all of us, feel that our trip was not in vain. The night before I returned to Little Rock, Mother and I embraced one another and talked about old times. She and I had shared moments together that she and I would never forget, and for that reason, we cried a little, then we talked a little. As I prepared to leave, Mother reached under her pillow, pulled out a package, and said, "Here, take this. You will need it to help you move back here." I took it without hesitation, because I knew it would offend her if I did otherwise. I gave thanks to the Lord for this tremendous blessing that he bestowed upon me and for helping me make the right decision to go home for Christmas.

I arrived in Little Rock Sunday night, and after sharing with Vicki bits and pieces about the trip, I handed her a cashier's check for her to deposit it into the account. She glanced at it nonchalantly. Then suddenly, her head did a double take in disbelief. After we had gone through twenty questions or so, Vicki could not believe what transpired during my trip. Finally, as the hour became late, we concluded the evening with a toast of sparkling non-alcoholic grape beverage, and she said, "All I have to say is that your mother must really love you a lot".

Chapter Fourteen

THE PRODIGAL SON RETURNS

We brought in the New Year (1986) in positive fashion. We were happier than we had been in many years, and our children, although they had never lived in Atlanta, were more than stimulated about moving there. The only things we dreaded leaving behind were our friends and our beloved St. John Baptist Church. Speaking of St. John, an arsonist set it on fire in 1985, which in turn, brought the church family even closer together.

Our pastor, Rev C.D. Edwards, devised a plan, with the help of others, and labeled it, "Sacrificial Giving". This plan, for the most part, called upon each individual to make his or her own sacrifice for the sake of the church. God had been so good to me and had answered my prayers earnestly, that I was more than happy to give St. John a pledge. In return, God blessed me again by touching the hearts of my brothers in Christ, enabling them to move us down to Atlanta free of charge. "PRAISE GOD!" God had shown me that if I would take a step for Him, He would take three for me, for it would have cost me three thousand dollars to move professionally.

We arrived in Atlanta on February 28, 1986; about six months after my grandmother had died. We moved into her house and put a few things in storage. Meanwhile, I tore down her old garage and put up a new one with a storage area.

Things were going just great, because I had been promised a job before even moving down there. However, that job was not to begin until April 1, which would give me plenty of time to move, finish the garage, and take a vacation. I did all of the above with pleasure, and when time came to go to work, I decided to take another job, than the one promised to me. This job was similar to the type of work I had been accustomed to, although the pay was not quite, as I had expected. I prayed unto the Lord, and had asked Him to bless me with the same type of job that I had had previously, but to exclude the racism, intimidation, bigotry, and hatred.

I worked for three months or more before realizing I had prayed for this job. I was slow to recognize it simply because of the pay, but oh, how everything began to fall into place. My supervisor's name was Billy, and he and his whole family were Christian people. This machining company belonged to their family, and they all ran it together. I had never seen anything quite like this and will probably never see another to match it.

These were hardworking people, and down-home and humble-minded. Some of us would sometimes go running together. We would and could talk about anything under the sun. Billy was a deacon in his church, and therefore, he knew a little about the scriptures. The liberties that I received at this job were sometimes unbelievable, but genuine in appearance. I could read or listen to the radio while working, take time off whenever needed, and receive as many phone calls or coffee breaks as needed. Of course, it took me a little time to make the adjustment, but eventually I fell right in with the swing of things.

Chapter Fifteen

THE MARCH ON FORSYTH COUNTY

from a marshal's perspective

Thus saith the Lord God of Israel, Let my people go,
that they may hold a feast unto me in the wilderness.
—Exodus 5:1

One day while listening to the radio at work, I heard that a man named Dean Carter and a few others were planning to march in Forsyth County to commemorate the death of Dr. Martin Luther King Jr., and show that blacks and whites could walk together in Forsyth County. Fear and intimidation had been quite evident for blacks in Forsyth County for seventy-five years. The reason for this fear initially occurred in 1912, on Sunday, September 18. Mae Crow, an eighteen-year old white girl was allegedly beaten and raped by three black youngsters named Ernest Knox, Ed Collins, and Oscar Daniels. Nearly one thousand blacks left their homes, farms, and property in Forsyth County because of this incident. Blacks in neighboring Dawson County ran for their lives also, and they never returned to these counties.

In 1980, Saturday, July 27, Miguel Marcelli, a black firefight from Atlanta, while attending a picnic in Forsyth, was shot in the neck. He survived the shooting, and two white men were found guilty for the first time in a crime against a black person.

In December of 1986, Chuck Blackburn announced a "Brotherhood March" to honor Dr. Martin Luther King Jr. From that point, he began to receive death threats on his life, family, and property. Suddenly, Blackburn withdrew plans to march. That is when signals began to get crossed, whether or not the march was on or off again. Dean Carter, a martial-arts instructor and construction worker, decided that the march must happen and so he took up the mantle. Dean contacted veteran civil rights leaders and City Councilman Hosea Williams, who on January 15, 1987, initiated plans to join Dean Carter in the march against fear, in spite of the numerous threats from the Ku Klux Klan.

After hearing these reports on the radio, the spirit man in me felt a compelling need to be there, but my flesh was weak with fear. Dr. King once said it is only human to be afraid, but it's inhuman to let fear impede progress. Therefore, I decided not to listen to those fears.

On January 17, 1987, the "March against Fear and Intimidation," took place in Forsyth County. There were approximately fifty marchers, who were violently attacked by several hundred angry whites, including members of the Klu Klux Klan. The Klan was established after the Civil

War, as a disguised society of white men, determined to reestablish and maintain white supremacy in the South. The original Klan was founded in Tennessee in 1867; and soon launched a campaign of terror against former slaves across the South. Their primary efforts, then, were to dissuade blacks from voting. The role by night was to conceal their identities beneath white sheets and masks to intimidate the whites that tried to take up black causes.

On January 19, 1987, the civil rights family announced plans to join the second march. I too, made up my mind to march regardless of the opposition, and that was final. Many others grappled with their conscience, and found it difficult to make a clear-cut decision as to whether or not they would participate in the march. Some prominent Atlantans were distressed by mixed emotions and by what some called political grandstanding. Mayor Andrew Young wrestled with his conscience all during that week, and said that he was concerned that the organizers of the march had not outlined specific long-term goals they wanted to achieve. However, at the last minute, the mayor finally decided to play a low-key role in the march.

Other local politicians felt compelled to participate, knowing that the eyes all over the globe were focused on them. People like Atlanta City Council president Marvin Arrington and Charles King of the Urban Crisis Center, had stated earlier that week, they had no intentions of attending the march. But after the march snowballed into an international historic event, not only did these two change their minds about attending the march, but Arrington decided to take his fifteen year old son to Forsyth. Arrington stated that he thought it would be beneficial for his son to get the flavor of what the movement entailed.

I must admit, as I look back at this encounter, it was truly a miraculous occasion. That fifty people, marching nonviolently, could trigger compassion and support from all over the world, is just unthinkable. However, just as Jesus fed the multitude of five thousand with two fish and five barley loaves, the Holy Spirit touched the hearts of thousands all over the nation, compelling them to make their presence known in the march.

Chapter Sixteen

A MESSAGE FROM GOD

Hosea called a rally the night before the march, and oh, what a rally it was. This miraculous event was sending off blessings left and right. Never before in twenty years had all of these Civil Rights leaders been able to come together on one accord and walk hand in hand. Now, somehow, the curse had been broken, and these leaders began to stand up for the dream, which seemingly was fading away into oblivion.

The platform was titled "Coalition to End Fear and Intimidation in Forsyth County". All these staff leaders were present and gave brief speeches, Mrs. Coretta Scott King, Dr. Joseph Lowery, Rabbi Alvin Sugarman, and Rev. C.T. Vivian. The rally was long and victorious, for we raised over thirty-one thousand dollars that night, which was used to pay for the buses Marta provided for us. Some of the old veterans of the movement gave us rules and regulations concerning the march, and several people signed up to be marshals, including me. After that, everybody went home and retired for the night, preparing to meet at the King Community Center at 7:30 a.m.

The next morning was beautiful and cool; another blessing from the Lord, for previously it had been frightfully cold and wet. People started gathering promptly at 7:30 a.m. and none was complaining. They were mainly concerned if they were in the right location. At 9:00 a.m., the march organizers began passing out orange-vested jackets for the marshal identification. We received instructions concerning the dos and don'ts before, during, and after the march.

By 9:15 a. m. a string of buses gathered for two blocks or more, down Auburn Avenue in front of the King Center facing downtown Atlanta. March organizers were amazed at the large number of people who had gathered within minutes and were showing no signs of dispersing. There were People, people, people many of them carrying banners and cardboard signs waiting to board the buses. As large as the crowd was, there seemed to be an unusual solemnity and obedience. They listened intently with order and patience to the bus marshals for boarding instructions. There was no singing or chanting, although a few did bring newspapers and books to read.

There appeared to be more than fifteen thousand waiting to board the buses, which was more people than available seats, leaving hundreds of potential marchers stranded. Six members of the NAACP chapter were forced to wait out the march at a restaurant on North Avenue. Along with the one hundred **Marta,** buses hired by City Councilman Hosea Williams, at a six-hour cost of twenty-two thousand dollars, were seventy more assorted buses from churches, schools, and private carriers.

At 10:50 a.m. organizers announced that, the buses were full, forcing hundreds of people to seek other ways to get to Forsyth County. Many managed to hitch rides with the more than two hundred private cars, vans, and trucks in the rear of the assembly. The buses left the King Center and reassembled at the Civic Center, and there we discovered hundreds more in search of a ride to Forsyth. Hosea Williams then had to hire more buses, and thank God, for the cab company that provided a hundred free taxicabs.

The forty-five minute wait at the Civic Center was painstaking for some, mainly because of uncomfortable positions, and having to go to the restroom. However, I did all I could on my bus, to keep the people from getting nervous and restless. For instance, we sang freedom songs, did a roll call, and I read them some literature on the Dr. King philosophy of non-violence. Through the course of our waiting, we found out that one of our marchers had been a participant in the first march on Forsyth. We had him to give us an exclusive report concerning its details.

Finally, at 11:30 a.m., the convoy headed out of the Civic Center onto the expressway. At one point, the convoy of rented Marta buses, faded peace vans, and private cars and buses stretched down three miles of Georgia 400, which was from Haynes Bridges Road in Alpharetta to the Holcomb Bridge Road ramp in Roswell.

While we were en route to Forsyth, David Duke, a former Ku Klux Klan leader, but now the president of NAAWP, began handing out leaflets and speaking to his supporters. A crowd soon gathered around him shouting, "White power," and, "Go home, nigger". GBI agents quickly surrounded the crowd and kept its members isolated from the larger gathering.

At that time, the convoy was about three or four miles from Cumming, Ga. Suddenly, David Duke got in his car, left the protesters, and met the convoy out on the expressway, but only he was blocking our passage. The convoy came to a halt for about twenty minutes, and very few had any idea of the trouble that was occurring up ahead. Although we saw several state troopers and GBI agents moving swiftly to the scene, we still did not know exactly what the trouble was. Later we found out that David Duke had been arrested for reckless conduct and illegally blocking a state highway.

The convoy was underway once more, and we finally reached our destination at 1:45 p.m. It took roughly one hour for the complete convoy to exit the expressway. The town swamped with traffic, ran out of parking space long before the convoy arrived. Air space was also at a premium, with eight law enforcement and press helicopters hovering overhead. The FFA had ordered all other air traffic away from the area. There was one incident, whereby a Georgia State Patrol helicopter had to chase away a small airplane.

News media had a field day covering this story, and a lot of would be shoppers canceled their plans and stayed at home to watch the news coverage on television. This march drew attention from not only the national media, but from foreign media as well, Canada, Sweden, and West Germany's media were all lending a watchful eye to this coverage. Thea Rosenbaum, producer for the German television network ARD, said, "We wouldn't miss this for the world." She and her

Washington, D.C., based crew were later joined by additional journalists and American reporters.

After climbing to the top of the bridge, each marshal was still assigned to his particular group. We gave the crowd instructions, and the march began soon thereafter. Scores of photographers, camera crews, preceded the marchers, while other reporters lined the path. At one point, seven helicopters jockeyed for position overhead, with media aircraft outnumbering those of law enforcement agencies. Media not only covered the news, but in some cases, they became a part of it. A black reporter, known as Cynthia Pryor, for television station WBRC in Birmingham, found herself and crew in the midst of a crowd of counterdemonstrators, while trying to tape a report. When the camera began rolling, she was showered with spit, fistfuls of mud and racial slurs.

As the peaceful marchers, about twenty-five thousand strong, marched silently down the spiraling road, ripples of recognition swept through the sea of onlookers. They nudged each other, pointing out some of the dignitaries like Mrs. Coretta Scott King, Hosea Williams, C.T. Vivian, Joseph Lowery, and others.

Counterdemonstrators had their own placards that expressed a certain intellect, such as, "GO HOME, NIGGER!" "FORSYTH WILL ALWAYS BE WHITE." The Confederate flags were waved, about fifty in all, some large and some small. The white protesters ran the gamut from mothers with young children to teenagers to grizzled men in baseball caps. Some of the men wore camouflage fatigues, while others wore jeans and T-shirts with jackets. Four men became apparent in the crowd of counterdemonstrators. They were members of the Invisible Empire Knights of the Ku Klux Klan, adorned in plain white robes, and pointed hoods.

Hit in the head by a brick, a man in the march was hospitalized due to the injury; and a young woman was medically treated after being struck with a lead pipe. Another person in the march received minor cuts when a group of whites smashed a concrete block into his car window. The Georgia Bureau of Investigation agents and guardsmen broke into the crowd of white protesters and immediately restored things to order, although one agent chased a young man who had spit on him, then tackled him in the mud, and shoved his face against a chain fence.

When the mile-long march ended at the courthouse, GBI agents were still making arrests amongst the white protesters. There were major differences in this movement from the movement of old. The movement, more than a decade ago, did not receive the support of the state and local enforcement agencies, but now these arrests were against whites opposing civil rights rather than against blacks demanding equality. This movement, *by-and-large*, was bi-racially mixed, which made a broad statement to the counterdemonstrators.

U.S. Senator, Sam Nunn, and Senator Wyche Fowler were present at the march accompanied by Assistant Attorney General William Bradford Reynolds to the courthouse.

Democratic presidential candidate, Gary Hart, an attendee, along with Congressman John Lewis, elected recently to fill Fowler's U.S. House seat. Congressman Lewis is a veteran of the civil rights movement. Therefore, he was obliged for the opportunity to speak to the marchers by saying, "I think by being here, you are saying that we will not tolerate racism, not in Forsyth County, not in Georgia, not anywhere in this country."

As the day wore on, speaker after speaker took the podium and made remarks. The never-ending crowd of marchers kept coming as the helicopters circled the area, continuously in low fashion. Hosea Williams was the closing speaker and his revelation knowledge revealed to others what God was saying, not only to the people of Forsyth County, but to people all over who practiced racism, bigotry, and hatred. He spoke from the book of Exodus 5:1 "Thus saith the Lord God of Israel, Let My People Go, that they may hold a feast unto ME in the wilderness." The noisy helicopters and counterdemonstrators did their best to drown out Hosea's brief speech, but God's Word went forth, piercing every ear.

It was 4:45 p.m., the rally had ended, and the sun was setting. The crowd poured hurriedly down the march's route, flanked by national Guardsmen. In all of their eagerness to retreat to the buses, people became separated from their original group. For that reason, some 250 marchers were stranded at a shopping center without buses, and were terrified at the thought of being in Forsyth County after dark.

In closing, I would like to say thank God for the Cumming's family, who stood out on their front porch, waving as we marched by, with an American flag flying from their house to boot. They were not afraid to stand up for what they thought was right. I am almost sure that there are others in Forsyth who are people of goodwill. Yet, we will never know who they are until they *stand and be counted*. Remember, my brothers and sisters, "It is human to be afraid, but it's inhumane to let fear impede progress".

The Author

Anthony L. Freeman is a philanthropist at heart, who has spent several years entertaining audiences from all walks of life. His most enjoyable moment of achievement was when he saw the tears from the eyes of the people who had received his message in song. Anthony at one time adopted the role of manager in food management, corporate president of Black & White, Esp., a booking agency, record producer, publisher, label owner, songwriter, recording artist, a stage performer, and speaker.

Anthony believes that it is teach individual's credit to recognize his or her God given talent and use it.

Because of the extravagance of those revelations, and so I would not get a big head, I was given the gift of a handicap to keep me in constant touch with my limitations.

2 Corinthians 12:7

LUST and Vain Glory is an autobiographical novel that gives witness to the Power of God and His Providence. The book reveals how only God can illuminate and transform a life that is misguided and polluted. What Anthony viewed as a handicap was in essence a gift from God that taught him patience and humility. This saga chronicles his close encounter with Death and Success. It is designed to captivate your mind with a sense of curiosity, situated with a degree of uncertainty. This book, as reported by its many readers, promises to touch your every emotion while simultaneously proposing a challenge to each individual.

Printed in the United States
By Bookmasters